xicancuicatl

Wesleyan Poetry

xicancuicatl

ALFRED ARTEAGA

COLLECTED POEMS

Edited by David Lloyd   Foreword by Cherríe Moraga

Wesleyan University Press   Middletown, Connecticut

Wesleyan University Press
Middletown CT 06459
www.wesleyan.edu/wespress

Manufactured in the United States of America.

Designed by Mindy Basinger Hill.

Typeset in 10.25/14 point Garamond Premier Pro.

Front cover art: "The Man Without Desire" (1988), by Gronk.
Acrylic on canvas, 73 ¼ x 61 ½ in. Courtesy of the artist
and Daniel Saxon Gallery.

Library of Congress Cataloging-in-Publication Data

Names: Arteaga, Alfred, 1950–2008, author.

Title: Xicancuicatl : collected poems / Alfred Arteaga.

Other titles: Poems

Description: Middletown, Connecticut : Wesleyan University Press, [2020]

Series: Wesleyan poetry | Includes bibliographical references and index.

Summary: "Xicancuicatl: Collected Poems is a comprehensive volume of poetry and prose poetry by the Chicano poet, Alfred Arteaga" — Provided by publisher.

Identifiers: LCCN 2020020402 (print) | LCCN 2020020403 (ebook) |
ISBN 9780819579690 (cloth) | ISBN 9780819579683 (trade paperback) |
ISBN 9780819579706 (ebook)

Subjects: LCGFT: Poetry.

Classification: LCC PS3551 .R726 2020 (print) |LCC PS3551 (ebook) |
DDC 811/.54—dc23

LC record available at https://lccn.loc.gov/2020020402

LC ebook record available at https://lccn.loc.gov/2020020403

5 4 3 2 1

PARA SUS HIJAS

CONTENTS

HOUSE WITH THE BLUE BED

RED

FRØZEN ACCIDENT

ACT ZERO

FOREWORD

"Time Stretched (Too) Thin"

CHERRÍE MORAGA

"TAKE THE INTERIOR OF ZERO,"
ALFRED ARTEAGA INVITES. AND I ENTER.

In the short two decades of knowing Alfred, I first met the pages of his work with a kind of awe; imaging him, The Poet, occupying the world of his myriad travels, languages, relationships, meetings, and departures with a certain bravado I never could've dreamed. I fantasized what it might be like to be that free—a large, light-skinned, and bearded man trotting the globe. But somehow Alfred always remained tethered to rest of us—the smaller in stature, the browner, the female—not by duty, but by the pure knowing he'd be lost without us. A humility embedded into the very heart of Alfred Arteaga's Xicanismo and poetry.

As Xicanxs we are always on the brink of a particular kind of disappearance. On both sides of the border, we are often an unacknowledged forgotten people whose right to be as we are is at times publicly questioned. Arteaga's poetry and criticism would name us again and again, as inheritors of the original impulse of American Literature—the flor y canto (in Xochitl, in Cuicatl) of the nahua scribes and their descendants. Like the hummingbird that "can fly backwards," Alfred was tasked to look back and in so doing conceived a multilingual Xicanx languaging which, in some way, anticipates a still unimaginable global future. This visionary collection of writings, which David Lloyd has faithfully brought into being, reflects the very mestizaje of Arteaga's imaginings, bound by an American Indigenous perspective where the temporal and spatial spiral off of one another to tell story as the body remembers it; where the elements remain elemental and where sand and ocean meet and wind crosses continents to bind and separate. Here fire is sex and arrow at once. Arteaga's work is unsurpassed in capturing the pure ephemerality and landed beauty that is Xicanx poetry spoken, danced, and painted.

◆

If the truth be told, it took me weeks to absorb the plethora of polylingual reflection and invention presented in this text. I read each of its nearly three hundred pages, employing my first-generation–educated English; a Spanish I'm only *half*-good at; a French I know nothing of; and a self-taught Nahuatl, fairly restricted to the Aztec pantheon of people and place. Still, reading *Xicancuicatl* felt wholly familiar in that the bifurcation and blending of languages *is* the Xicanx lingua franca in the Southwest, as it was in my own childhood home where Spanish and English and Spanglish traveled across four generations of comprehension.

This book is not one to easily consume. It requires at least a good month's reading, where one might turn (and re-turn) to a passage every few days or so to allow the lines to reside within the reader, and perhaps change the reader for the better, the truer. This is the work and hope of literature—language that resonates within a person to such a degree that it generates meaning from what before had seemed meaningless.

There is much to consider here in these pages from within and without. In Arteaga's Xicanx imagination there are no borders—from ocean to ocean, from Berkeley to Belfast or Ben Bulben. Meanwhile, the poet concedes, *geopolitical borders break bodies*. He writes of touch and its relationship to power. How is the border between the untouchables and the touched created?

He asks—*Who gets touched? Who matters? Who doesn't get touched or is touched too late?*

Xicancuicatl creates a portrait of Aztlán and its citizens in the act of touching across time and place—from the Chicano Moratorium of 1970 in East Los Angeles to a gathering among Chicano and Chicana artists and poets in San Francisco some twenty-five years later. Arteaga describes that mid-1990s moment as our "Chicano Renaissance." (I, too was in attendance.) His celebration of artists and writers paradoxically presaged the illnesses and deaths of many of those celebrated that evening. Perhaps as Xicanx artists, this is the foundation of our "dislocasia." "Displaced from a time line," Alfred called the dis-ease. Did he mean history?

◆

To allow Alfred Arteaga's work to enter you is to be transported into the wholeness of zero; that timeless site that one may find in the most grounded of meditative moments. To read this work is to enter that site; to be animated with consciousness in an awakened sensorial body. It is to recognize the ephemeral location of spirit and its ever-presence. It is to read and write and live in anticipation of your own road home to the underworld of Mictlan.

The poet writes, "sé bien de dónde vengo y más o menos / a qué hora acabaré . . ."

Did he? Did Alfred, as tlamatini, know the hour of his death? That "hue of time stretched [so suddenly] thin" in his own life?

Time and space.

In this book, Alfred writes before the edge of the world, the Pacific looking West.

I, too, join him there and watch the waves return and recede, to and from our shared California homeland.

7 Deciembre 2019
Santa Bárbara / Anisq'oyo

INTRODUCTION

Alfred Arteaga, Poet of Crossing

DAVID LLOYD

> These cantos chicanos begin with an X and end with an X. They are examples of xicano verse, verse marked with the cross, the border cross of alambre y río, the cross of Jesus X in Native America, the nahuatl X in méxico, mexicano, xicano. It is our mark, our cross, our X, our sign of never ceasing to be born at the point of two arrows colliding, X, and at the gentle laying of one line over another line, X.
> *Alfred Arteaga, "X antecanto: the xicano sign"*[1]

ANDO XICANDO

Alfred Arteaga was among the most innovative of a rich generation of Xicanx poets writing from the 1980s through the first decade of the twenty-first century. His work, indeed, is unimaginable outside the upsurge of Xicanx cultural and political activism that began to take shape in the 1960s. Born in East Los Angeles in 1950, Arteaga was a teenager in 1965 when the Civil Rights movement reached its height and the Civil Rights Act was signed, and as the protests against the Vietnam War were gaining force and intensity. The convergence of anti-racist and anti-imperialist organizing found expression in the rise of the Chicano movement in the late 1960s and the Chicano Moratorium of 1970, a major protest by Xicanx war veterans and their allies against the war. While a student at East Los Angeles College, Arteaga covered the Moratorium as a young journalist freelancing for the *Los Angeles Free Press* and participated in the flourishing cultural and political upsurge of "La Raza," the Xicanx people, before leaving in 1974 to do an MFA at Columbia University in New York. He returned to California and taught at San José City College before beginning a PhD on William Shakespeare and Sor Juana de la Cruz at the University of California, Santa Cruz in 1982. After graduating in 1987, apart from three years as a professor at the University of Houston he spent most of the rest of his life in the Bay Area of Northern California.

His appointment in 1990 in the Department of English at the University of California, Berkeley, coincided with a new moment of organizing for the desegregation of the university, which the Xicanx and other social movements had initiated. That moment also saw the hardening of reactionary efforts to roll back affirmative action, which had been a partial remedy for generations of discriminatory hiring and admissions practices. In the fall of 1997, in the wake of the UC Regents' ending of affirmative action, Arteaga's department denied him tenure in what he described as "an ugly display of discrimination and retaliation" (*House with the Blue Bed*, #25), despite his brilliant and pioneering critical work *Chicano Poetics*, which Cambridge University Press published in 1997, and the innovative poetry that is collected here. Arteaga's determination not to acquiesce quietly to an act of manifest discrimination was not only a necessary personal decision but also a principled act of political resistance to conservative efforts to contain and limit the democratization of the university. He undertook an ultimately successful law suit against the university that led to his reappointment in 1998 in the Department of Ethnic Studies, where he continued his work as a much loved and respected teacher of poetry and of Chicano Studies. But the stresses and strains of his struggle seem to have taken a heavy toll on his health, and for the last decade of his life, even as he continued to produce some of his most significant poetic work, he suffered from a series of heart attacks that eventually proved fatal. He died in July 2008 after a brief spell in hospital.

Arteaga's life coincided with a crucial period in the formation of Xicanx culture and with the emergence of the distinctive modes of poetic writing that he theorized so cogently in *Chicano Poetics*. As a poet and a critic he always retained a grateful and gracious sense of his relation and his debt to the larger context of Xicanx cultural inventiveness whose vitality he knew at first hand. In conversation with his thinking as a brilliant literary theorist and critic, Arteaga's poetry demonstrated a considerable singleness of purpose and consistency, while his work as a whole unfolded in a long and steady arc from first to last. His published poetic volumes, from which this collection is mostly composed, included *Cantos* (1991), a sequence of lyrical and quasi-epic poems; *House with the Blue Bed* (1997), a blend of prose and poetry that forms a kind of non-linear autobiography; and the extended prose poem *Love in the Time of Aftershocks* (1998). These were followed by three further volumes of poetry in Spanish and English, or, better put, in Spanish and English and a mixture of Spanish and English often seeded with French, Nahuatl, and other languages: *Red* (2000); the dense and ambitious volume *Frøzen Accident* (2006); and his final, posthumous volume, *Act Zero* (2008), which my own small press Cusp Books had been working on with him just before he died. He was a poet who made crucial breakthroughs in the language of poetry, a poet whose formal resources and finely tuned ear for sound patterns and language play were quite remarkable. The tribute made to him by the late French philosopher Gilles Deleuze, that he was "among those rare poets who are able to raise or shape a new language within their language," is entirely pertinent.[2] Yet Arteaga never lost sight of the sources of his own linguistic experiments in the polylingual context of Xicanx culture in the US Southwest, a phenomenon of which he writes extensively in his critical work and which forms the major shaping impulse of his poetic language.

Indeed, Arteaga's poetic work, from *Cantos* on, not only draws from but steadily extends his critical explorations of Xicanx writing, making the whole body of his work an ongoing dialogue between his deep knowledge of and reflections on the traditions of Xicanx writing and his own poetic practice. The thematic unity of the poetry with the critical work affirms that Arteaga's criticism was also an act of self-understanding and self-definition. His body of poetical work pursues a consistently unfolding project, which sought not only to draw on the history and rhetoric of Xicanx writing from that of the eighteenth-century poet and nun Sor Juana de la Cruz to the works of his contemporaries, such as Alurista, Francisco X. Alarcón, Lorna Dee Cervantes, Cherríe Moraga, Gloria Anzaldúa, and Juan Felipe Herrera (all of whom he discusses in *Chicano Poetics*), but also to explore the forms and conditions of *Xicanidad*, Xicanx-ness. As his continual emphasis on process rather than on any mode of fixed identity suggests, it was not so much an ontology of the Xicanx, a *Ser*, that he sought, but an exploration of the condition of Xicanidad as a continual becoming. As he wrote in *Chicano Poetics*, "It is not a state of being but rather an act, xicando, the progressive tense, ando xicando, actively articulating the self."[3] In the critical field, indeed, *Chicano Poetics* represents, as *Cantos* does in the formation of contemporary Xicanx poetry, an exploration less of "identity," cultural or political, than of the conditions and resources of *mestizaje*, hybridity and polyglossia. Both works frame what would always be Arteaga's enduring commitment, the investigation and development of poetic resources grounded in the fundamentally intercultural and interlingual condition of the Xicanx. Arteaga's project, in both his poetry and his critical writing, is a sustained reclamation of the foundations of Xicanx poetics in our historical situation of radical heteroglossia and is, so far as I am aware, still virtually the only work of this rhetorical orientation and theoretical sophistication carried out in the field. In its concern with hybridized cultural formations, it is most immediately comparable to Caribbean Anglophone and Francophone work on creole culture, and has particular resonance with poet-critics such as Édouard Glissant, Kamau Brathwaite, and M. NourbeSe Philip, especially her experiments in formalizing creolization for her first volume, *She Tries Her Tongue*.

XICANCUICATL

While deeply cognizant of the traditions of Xicanx and Latin American writing from which he drew, Arteaga's inaugural book-length work *Cantos* was still an extraordinarily precocious and ambitious first collection, as its very title suggests. Alluding quite evidently to the epic models of Dante Alighieri's *Divine Comedy* and Ezra Pound's *Cantos*, as well as to Pablo Neruda's *Canto General*, which is cited in the very first poem, *Cantos* also quietly invokes a no less venerable and continuous tradition of epic cantos in its samplings of the medieval Spanish romance *Poema de Mio Cid* and of Gaspar Pérez de Villagrá's *La Historia de la Nueva México* (1610) in several of its four opening cantos.[4] These poems, as the wealth and variety of Arteaga's allusions suggest, are unabashedly erudite, but they absorb that erudition into a lyrical forward movement that is capable of transforming semiotic play into sensuality and interlingual punning into street wit. Many of the poems embed his erudition at a much deeper level: in his intimate knowledge of Spanish and Latin American writing, and in his understanding of a lyrical impulse that continues to underwrite the political force of so much of modern Spanish-language writing (one thinks of Miguel Hernández in Spain or César Vallejo's posthumous *España, aparta de mí este cáliz*, as well as of Neruda, who was clearly one of Arteaga's early influences).

Cantos constantly deploys allusions to articulate a rich but always provisional hybrid subjectivity. Its deployment of Spanish, English, French, Nahuatl, and German is not merely the postmodern play of pastiche but is embedded in Arteaga's understanding of the history of recurrent and ever more complicated forms of *mestizaje* that constitute the culture and subjectivity of Mexican Americans. Like the French philosopher Jean-Luc Nancy, who contributed an important essay to Arteaga's edited critical volume *An Other Tongue*, he understands *mestizaje* not as a state, but as a process, and that understanding of process informs the most lyrical and moving moments of the *Cantos*.[5] The result is a volume that formally recasts the epic of foundation into the process of continual hybridization, converting identity into the risky adventure of "crossing"—crossing borders, crossing cultures, crossing languages—whose figure, as Arteaga's introductory note affirms, is at once the "Chi" or "X" of Xicanx popular culture and the chiasmus of the rhetorician, "the trope of the cross and opposition."[6] *Cantos* is also a volume that, while alluding to the epic tradition of foundational long poems, refuses both totalization and foundation even as it rejects the formation of a national language or myth: the initial cantos, with their grand historical sweep from Columbus's so-called discovery and the subsequent brutal Spanish conquest and colonization of the Americas to contemporary alambristas, the migrant workers who crisscross the US–Mexican border, give way to a medley of other forms, corridos, romances, prose poems, and epistles.

Mixing or medley is, of course, not only the thematic preoccupation of the work, with its record of colonial hybridization of bodies, languages, and cultures in the Spanish and US colonizations of an indigenous world. It is also a formal procedure, one that Arteaga roots in Xicanx speech and poetics, describing it not as a mere assemblage of citations from different sources and languages, but as "an interlingual style that emphasizes the form of the form."[7] Arteaga's insistence in *Cantos* on citation, multilingualism, and "heteroglossia" points towards his long-standing interest in the Soviet critic Mikhail Bakhtin's formal and stylistic analyses of epic and novel as genres, though Arteaga rejects Bakhtin's contention that in contrast to the novel, which is defined by its multiple and competing voices, lyric poetry is the "monolingual" province of the single voice. Xicanx poetry, including his own, dialogizes lyric and defies the authority of the single voice, which is that of the master and the state.[8] Bakhtin's terminology—heteroglossia, monoglossia, hybridization—informs Arteaga's poetics and his rhetorical analyses, the terms by which he situates Xicanx poetry in its larger cultural and political contexts. Xicanx writing and culture are the products of a layered history of conquests through which the subordinated cultures have not so much been eliminated or erased as displaced and hybridized. Linguistically, this expresses itself in the interlingual play of *caló*, a hybrid vernacular language that mobilizes Spanish and English elements, and in the deployment of varying amounts of Spanish, Nahuatl, and English in the literary work. The often subversive juxtaposition of languages that highlights varying relations of authority among them (as, for example, the different valence of Spanish as a language of the state in Mexico and a language of the subaltern in the United States), and the grammatical hybridization of their lexicons, generate an active process of interlingual sampling and mixing that is intrinsic to Xicanx culture.

Caló, working at the ragged interfaces of languages that rub up against one another along the political and cultural borderlands that constitute Aztlán, furnishes the exemplary "form of the form" for Arteaga's inventive language play in *Cantos* and later volumes. Arteaga takes as an example of caló José Montoya's use in his poem "El Louie" of the word "*shinadas*," shined or polished, which is a hybrid of English "shine" and a Spanish plural past participle, "-adas."[9] *Cantos* extends the "form of the form" of caló, juxtaposing different languages of authority with vernacular idiom, national and institutional languages of power with the languages of the subordinated. Typical is "Corrido Blanco," a poem based on Sor Juana's famous *Respuesta* to the bishop who advised her, as a woman, not to write:

Her notebook declares, "If for you fathers
My logos suffers too, (what did Paul say?)
'Mulieres' You 'in Ecclesia tace-
ant.' Too, mujeres en iglesia, you

te nacen, palabrita, tú, mía."
In the schools from Rome, you are born living,
From London too: nace la palabra.
And you become and kill a tongue or two.

The poem mixes Greek and Latin, the authoritative languages of the colonial and patriarchal Church, with translation into Spanish (and into the English of a monolingual United States that seeks to silence the bilingual Xicanx boy who appears in the third stanza). In some respects, the multilingual form of poetic language is Arteaga's response to the colonial imperative to silence "other tongues." But the poem also embeds a less evident language play, as Arteaga works an aural, interlingual pun on You, Too, two, and tú, making of the one tongue of monolingual institutions the supplementary two of dialogism (and tacitly invoking the unvoiced "tu" of a third language, French, both "killed" and "silenced" as well as the second person pronoun).[10] The language of the poem thus unsettles the authority of the monolingual by making the borders between languages unstable and uncertain so that one may no longer know in what language one is reading or speaking.

The possibilities of such linguistic crossings are explored with virtuosity in the second canto, "Textos vivos," which gives the pattern for a mode of poem that he continued to experiment with throughout his career:[11]

Entre las manos extiendes la red
from one hand to the other que lees,

desde una mano, one to another,
la red extiende, hoja colorada no
suelta, la red extendida y colorada
from one hand to the other que ves,
l'outre-vie du texte, outre-texte,
que lees, la red que detienes
al momento, that you read
entre estas dos manos
vivas

The movement in and out of distinct languages, Spanish, English and French, is counterpointed here by another elaborate interlingual pun, between *red* (Spanish for "net") and *red* (English color red), complicated by the fact that "la red colorada" is not, as the monolingual English speaker might infer from what seems a familiar word, a *colored* net, but a *red* net. The play between the net of the text—a further pun on text and textile that operates across all these languages—and the red of the lettering (which almost certainly alludes to the red inks used in the Aztec codices ("rojoglífico," as the poem has it a few lines later) establishes a network between languages that is there, in another tacit pun, to be read. Rhythmically, the restless enjambments of the thirty-one–line stanza mime the movement of eye and hand across the pages in a continuous doubling of reading and touching or threading of the text.

Citing the first stanza of the first canto—"A line, half water, half metal"—Arteaga once stressed the relation between his own compositional practice and the most common trope in Nahuatl poetry, *difrasismo*, that is, "the means of representing something in the coupling of two elements." Not surprisingly, "perhaps the most well known difrasismo is that for poetry, *in xochítl in cuicatl*, flower and song."[12] *Difrasismo* is not merely a specific trope drawn from the Nahuatl poetics of pre-conquest indigenous peoples, but the principle of what Arteaga sees as a distinctive Xicanx poetic procedure, including that of his own work. As the title of the essay "Mestizaje/Difrasismo" implies, both the process of mixing and the trope itself perform the dissolution of borders and boundaries where the two elements invoked infuse one another. If a phrase like *in xochítl in cuicatl* seems to reflect the tendency of Nahuatl speaking peoples to think in terms of dualities, as Miguel León-Portilla and others have claimed, Arteaga's reworking of *difrasismo* operates within the very terrain of poetic language to make dualities blur and tremble across the thresholds of division.[13] The concluding stanza of the second canto "Textos vivos" seems to cite a series of Nahuatl *difrasismos* only to disseminate them through a tour de force multilingual play:

tlilli in quecholli	[soot and flamingo]
tlilli in tlapalli	[soot and blood]
in ixochiuh in xronotopxopan	[her flower and "spring chronotope"]
xiuhtlacuilolli ya amoxcalitec	[year-paintings (or chronicles) and libraries]
krugozory:	[world-view (Russian)]
xicancuicatl	[Xicanx song (neologism from Xicano and cuicatl, song)]

While some of these phrases seem to derive directly from Nahuatl, the first two probably intended to reference the black and red inks in the glyphs of those codices invoked earlier in the poem, as the stanza develops, Arteaga folds in a richer set of interlingual exchanges.[14] For instance, "xronotopxopan," which in this context looks like a Nahuatl word, fuses the Nahuatl xopan, or Spring (which can also form a *difrasismo* with cuicatl, or song, to designate a particular genre of poetry) with Bakhtin's Russian term *xronotop*, which is really a Russianization of the Greek *chronos* (Χρόνος, time) and *topos* (τόπος, space or place), another kind of *difrasismo,* translated into English as chronotope, literally a "time-space." The invocation of the shifting times and spaces through which Xicanx culture and poetics have emerged out of an indigenous context through successive colonial displacements and the imposition of layers of imperial languages is crucial to Arteaga's mapping of the material foundations of a specifically Xicanx worldview, lodged in displacement and hybridity rather than any fixed identity. This is what Bakhtin termed a *krugozor*, a very particular conceptual horizon through which the world is refracted.[15] That conceptual horizon is "Chicano poetics" or what Arteaga calls, in a beautiful and climactic *difrasismo,* xicancuicatl, Xicanx song.

DISLOCASIA

Arteaga's books immediately after *Cantos* largely took the form of prose poetry, which allowed him a new kind of processive writing within which to explore the hybrid constitutions of subjectivity. *Love in the Time of Aftershocks* and

House with the Blue Bed counterpoise a reclamation of desire and love against the unshirked force of temporal instability and displaced lives. First published as a separate chapbook and then reprinted in *Red*, the sequence *Love in the Time of Aftershocks* takes the event of the 1994 Los Angeles earthquake as a metaphor for the dynamics of urban life, as well as for the erotic shock of intimate relationship. The eight sections narrate what we might call a series of fractal fractures, aligning the most intimate rhythms of daily life and relation—sleeping, breathing, waking, desiring, touching—with the utterly impersonal forces that shape the landscape of Arteaga's birth city and region, the restless if imperceptible shifts of the tectonic plates in geological time:

> In the undulations of surface taken for still in the moment of present, as present, fluctuations in space so that up and down are simultaneously beside one another: that is Lomas, sheets of curved space, a surface that fights you and holds you and sets you up, she knows, like the valley but its negation, in affirmation of sky instead of the valley's emulation of hell and tectonic underpinnings, the *semper obscura* of the beneath and core. Simple, she believes in her simple act of taking in air and expelling air in rhythm she is making life in a progressive tense, in an idealization of invisible air, a palpable, sensible body of body. [IV]

The jittery prose form that Arteaga invents for this work, with its clipped syntax, paratactic jointures of phrase and matter, and its almost breathless onward movement, seems to enact the work's preoccupation with the shock and misalignment of encounter and "the attendant sense of dislocation [that] defies the law of the single whole." [III] *Love in the Time of Aftershocks* finds the form to map, through brief segments of dispersed tales in a single cross section of human and geological time, what it is to inhabit the multiple and often disjointed scales of world and earth.

House with the Blue Bed takes up the form not so much of the prose poem but of what the French would call the *récit*: a series of short and interconnected narratives that refuse chronological order, it constitutes a deep reflection on temporality and displacement, unsettling autobiographical certainty and composing the narrator in a shifting field of interweaving stories that mingle memory and meditative digressions. Straying from the beaches of Texas to those of Sligo, Ireland, and Baja California, from Berkeley to Barcelona or Belfast, and from Los Angeles to London and Mexico City, the twenty-six sections also shuttle back and forth through the narrator's life, from boyhood to the present, as memory and association dictate. Its meandering movement across space and time maps the interchanges of ad hoc and provisional moments of community with a pervasive sense of displacement and erotic longing, punctuated with moments of accidental or state-sanctioned violence. This sequence conjoins Arteaga's experience as a young freelancer for the *Los Angeles Free Press* covering the protests of the Chicano Moratorium, during which *Los Angeles Times* journalist Rubén Salazar was murdered by the police in the Silver Dollar Café, with his visit to Belfast and the grave of Bobby Sands, who died during the Irish Republican hunger strike of 1981. Foregrounding movement and encounter, the work explores the question of finding home and relationship in the distant, the lure of specificity of place and community vis-à-vis the openings of travel and the provisional communities that displacement affords. It expands into a narrative principle Arteaga's definition of "chicanismo" as being "at the site where social forces converge" and "as a dynamic of being in relation to others."[16] At its core is the experience that Arteaga so beautifully describes in "days" as *dislocasia*, an almost Proustian sensation of no longer knowing where or *when* one is:

> Dislocasia's characteristic sense of nonlocatability and of being lost seems to me more profound than merely spatial. True, it manifested itself first and foremost as a break in contiguity, as a break in the sense of place, but it always made me feel as if I were displaced from a time line, as if the reason for the dislocation in space were caused in the first instance by a fall from the flow of one time to another.

One could say that dislocasia is the subjective apprehension of the experience of displacement and the constant habitation of the interface that constitutes the condition of Xicanidad: this is what *House with the Blue Bed* explores through one individual's serial displacements and in its own idiosyncratic manner and prose.

Red was the collection in which Arteaga returned to lyric forms, and that volume in many ways represents a powerful synthesis of the two gravitational pulls on his work, contemporary US experimental poetics and the more lyrical traditions of Latin American verse. While it is a constant and yet remarkable feature of Arteaga's work that he remains open to these somewhat contradictory pulls, *Red* is not merely synthetic, an uneasy compromise between two traditions that engross him, but yet again the discovery of a new appropriate language. Our current moment of recrudescent white supremacy, state terror, and endless warfare probably makes it incumbent on poets of any seriousness to address in their work the ongoing drive to achieve technological mastery of the world and the racial violence of dispossession and accumulation which have characterized one red thread that runs through the history of the New World. But for a poet coming out of the colonial experience of Latin America and the Southwest the imperative is all the more charged. Arteaga was clearly pursuing in these poems a language that would suffuse the "hard" and prosaic language of abstraction with a humane language of passion that yet counts the cost of the violent histories that inform it.

Red is also imbued even more than the previous volumes with a sense of the urgency of its political moment and of the erosion of the advances gained in the multicultural push of the 1980s, as the verse speech "Tomorrow Today" and the poems "Lebensraum" and "Prayer for the Death of the Soul" most clearly reflect. These poems and the volume as a whole (published in 2000) were, after all, written through and in response to the racist campaigns that brought California in 1994 the statewide referendum for Proposition 187, which sought to deny public services to undocumented immigrants, and in 1996 for Proposition 209, the so-called "California Civil Rights Initiative," which sought to roll back affirmative action in state and state-funded institutions. It was also in this context of resurgent racism that the Regents of the University of California voted in 1995 to abolish affirmative action programs throughout the university system. These three poems, and in particular "Tomorrow Today," respond directly to an environment of militant white supremacy and the wedge politics that sought to create division among the ethnic groups differently affected by each successive measure. Twenty-five years later these poems have only gained in relevance and impact.

Arteaga could hardly have anticipated in his writings the very direct effect of the Regents' affirmative action decision on his own career. Two years later, the English Department at UC Berkeley would deny him tenure in a move that seemed to his students, and to the colleagues who protested this most anomalous decision, to be an expression of white backlash against the hiring of minority faculty that had gradually taken place in the 1980s. This backlash led, in the wake of the Regents' vote, to an effective purging of professors of color from UC Berkeley and other universities around the nation. Though he fought to retain his position and pursued a lengthy and finally successful lawsuit against the University of California, there is little doubt that the stresses of that attack on his work and his career played some part in precipitating the heart ailments that plagued him for the remaining decade of his life.

Despite the direct political address of these poems, however, *Red* is not a reactive or purely occasional volume. The larger contours of the work gathered in that book stake a different claim for a world that radically defies ethnic majoritarianism and the state-sponsored monoculturalism that *Chicano Poetics* devastatingly critiqued. That claim is enacted in part through interlinguality (once again via the contrary and sometimes jarring imperatives and resonances of English, Spanish, French, and German), and in part through poems like the three long metaphysical lyrics that comprise the third section, "Silvas Humanas," written in a limpid Spanish that establishes Arteaga as a versatile bilingual writer. *Red* pushes beyond its particular political moment to imagine and instantiate the more inclusive language and sensibility requisite to living in a genuinely multicultural society.

SONGS OF FLIGHT

Despite serious health problems, Arteaga never ceased to push the boundaries of his own poetic language. *Frøzen Accident*, his penultimate volume and the last published during his lifetime, continued his meditation on the dialogical relation of domination and conquest, survival and resistance, between Europe and the "New World." It also returned to some of the preoccupations and materials of *Cantos*, whose synthetic ambitions it shares in many ways. Its central poem, "Nezahualcoyotl in Mictlan," is a sequence of lyrics which, drawing in some part from Dante's *Inferno* and in general from the classical European motif of the descent into Hades, narrates the journey of Nezahualcoyotl, the philosopher king of Texcoco, into Mictlan, the Nahuatl "Region of the Dead." Nezahualcoyotl wrote the most renowned poetry of the preconquest Americas, including "Song of the Flight," a poem of exile written, when he was sixteen, after the assassination of his father Ixtlilxochitl, Lord of Texcoco. Arteaga invokes this poem directly in "Canto of Flight," the fifth poem of the sequence.[17] But although Arteaga seems to have absorbed some of the Nahuatl poet's mournful preoccupation with the transience of human existence, the journey to Mictlan has no obvious parallel in Nezahualcoyotl's surviving work and represents Arteaga's own synthetic rendering of a theme that bridges the mythic imaginaries of the old and the new world. In that respect, the volume as a whole has a focused concern with the violent confluence of Europe and the Americas, figured in the sequence's opening section as San Francisco, point where everything comes together: "given body there" ("Freezing Point"). That place is at once the cultural and geographical intersection of Europe and America, the western reach of Europe's expansive drive, and the West of the symbolic quadrant of cardinal points in Nahuatl cosmology, the western region that is colored red. From this point of intersection, or crossing, the narrator, personified as the "questioning poet" Equis (X), descends into Mictlan, a cold, northern land that seems a shadow of San Francisco, where "sky is fog, fog billows here" ("Mictlan"). He is accompanied in his journey by mysterious guides, first Gato and then Xeritzin, comparable respectively to the Greeks' Charon and Dante's Virgil. The sequence ends hauntingly with Xeritzin leading the way:

> to where there in the snow,
> the face of a woman lies
> perfect face, this poet,
>
> dark hair, pale lips and a white skin
> lost in snow . . .
> ["Marie Uguay"]

This dead poet is identified as Marie Uguay, the Montreal francophone poet, whose writings and whose early death from cancer at twenty-six seem to have haunted Arteaga since the *Cantos*, where her book *L'outre-vie* is cited several times.[18]

The sequence offers no consolation, however, concluding with the desolate image of the poet-quester covering up a "perfect face" with snow. Yet at the same time it stakes a powerful if deeply ambivalent claim for poetry. Apparently drawing on Nezahualcoyotl's own belief that living things are in fact no more than the paintings produced by Tloqueh Nahuaqueh, "The Giver of Life" and "The Lord of the Near and the Far," Arteaga returns constantly in the poem to "the inks that draw life from the dead," the red and the black of the codices, "for only in / codices do bodies truly animate."[19] But this conceit hardly permits an unambiguous celebration of poetic power and creativity: whatever power to preserve and commemorate poetry may claim, it remains a fictive power and an ephemeral song, a *floricanto* marking the difference that is the threshold of division and becoming:

> know this, you come to life
>
> in the cantos I sing, your acts
> your body, so many petals lying
> on white sand, gain color
> but not fact, in the poems, your line,

its cross, and the points it divides
are simple fact and not true,
for it is the flower and the song
that marks the sole zero,

that marks difference, not one. ["Aristotle"]

Whether or not "her breath // is bright fog or verbal reflection / of codex ink," Marie Uguay's "perfect face" is finally covered again in the white blank of snow. Poetry, it seems, exists at the intersection of persistence and ephemerality, presence and fading. It is hard not to read this complex and often disconsolate sequence without contemplating the probability that much of it was written out of Arteaga's successive near-fatal illnesses and his awareness of the probable imminence of his own death. That can only make the steady gaze it casts on mortality and its finality at once more daunting and more admirable.

"Nezahualcoyotl in Mictlan" stands on its own as a singular poetic achievement, but at the same time it is woven by recurring images and echoing phrases into the body of *Frøzen Accident* as a whole. The volume was clearly conceived as a fully integrated work, opening with the terse philosophical lyrics of "Derrida and Wittgenstein" and concluding with the "peninsular cityscape" of "California no es isla." In some sense then, in keeping with the epic ambitions of much of Arteaga's verse, the work takes the form of a poem of foundations and of emplacement. In a deeper sense, however, the volume as a whole is also a poem of endings, of California as the rim or edge at which the European project of civilization and empire meets its end, a culmination of history, so that for the European as once for the Aztec empire, the question becomes that of what it means to inhabit an end to history, a faltering of developmental time. Europe's flight into the New World is doubled in and by Nezahualcoyotl's Dantesque song—the two epics enfold one another at the same time as they point towards the poetic possibilities that lie beyond the contest of civilizations. In this volume, Arteaga likewise pushes his own linguistic explorations into a new and deeply implicit hybridity, where the border between words becomes a space of figural meeting and fusing, as in the opening sequence where words blur and blend like color bands on litmus paper: "figures mark / how natural sign bleeds / colors tear spread loose," or "an / arc flesh flushed / hunger rings from night." The language itself enacts the sorts of fusion and slippage among signs that at a larger level takes place between the Nahuatl and the European figures that inhabit the poem.

This section of the book and the last ("California no es isla") mark vividly how Arteaga's work continued to be imaginatively informed by his readings both in the history and culture of the indigenous Americas and by his sustained interest in European theory. Derrida's text on Europe, *L'autre cap*, is an important presence behind Arteaga's refiguring of San Francisco's peninsular geography, drawing as it does on Derrida's play with the notion of Europe as headland, *cap*, point and heading or direction:

> Europe is not only a geographical headland and heading that has always given itself the representation or figure of a spiritual heading, at once as project, task or infinite—that is to say, universal—idea, as the memory of itself that gathers and accumulates itself, capitalizes upon itself, in and for itself. Europe has confused its image, its face, its figure and its very place, its taking place, with that of an advanced point, the point of a phallus if you will, and thus, once again, with a heading for world civilization or human culture in general.[20]

Any more extended reading of *Frøzen Accident* would have to engage with Arteaga's dialogue with Derrida, as indeed any substantial approach to Arteaga's work will have to counterpoint an appreciation for the degree to which he drew on the rich resources of Xicanx and Nahuatl culture and traditions combined with his constant preoccupation with Europe, both as brutal fact of conquest and colonization, and as idea. For Arteaga, the being of the Xicanx could not be thought through without taking on board the coercive graft of indigenous roots with European colonization. The idea of Europe as the exemplar of civility and intellectual capital legitimated the bloody and genocidal conquest of the Americas. It continues to shape, despite every effort at desegregation, the idea of the university that sought to deny Arteaga and other academics of color tenure and to dismiss the work of poets like him as minor or marginal. Yet he seems always to have known, from his witty poem "The Small Sea of Europe" in *Cantos* to "Derrida and Wittgenstein" in *Frøzen Accident*, that any aesthetic or poetic reckoning with the conditions of Xicanx being would have to engage with the torque that colonialist European power had given to the emergence of the Americas as a site of crossing—linguistic, cultural and material. There are few contemporary poets who have achieved so singular a synthesis or syncretic exploration of the historical and cultural conditions of their work, or done so in a language so innovative and saturated as Arteaga achieves in the long arc of his work that culminates in *Frøzen Accident*.

Arteaga's final, posthumous volume *Act Zero* was at once a distillation and an extension of his various poetic strategies of *mestizaje* and linguistic crossings, comprising brief multilingual lyrics that foreground fluidity and non-identity, to the extent that at moments one cannot quite tell in which language any given word is to be read, as in "panes and fishes" / "pains and fishes," in "Sin Control"; a long lyric in Spanish; two linked meditative prose poems; and a pair of transcendently ethereal lyrics. Flight and flux are the book's motifs, within a poetic language that embraces so deeply its incarnation that it regains an almost innocent playfulness, which is nonetheless in deadly earnest. The concluding poem in the volume, "Chrome Yellow, Smooth, Echo," fittingly opens with "come home, a cross," resuming in one deft line the contrary impulses of Arteaga's work, suspended between homing and the constant crossing that he defined as the being of the Xicanx in the borderlands. The prose stanza that follows the opening lyric lines seems to condense in "the recollection of agony," a passage through or across both emotional and physical duress, for which the ailments of the heart are an all too chilling metaphor:

> each sole inch of darkness, after all, could have held whatever imagined: one cold heart of iron pounded to steel, hurled in sharp points: a cloth of so many tears revealing a cross section of sponge, yet flesh, yet blood. For that war is scar only. That smoke more dust on dirt only. It has been settled. The heart cannot be rebroken.

The striking simplicity of Arteaga's late poetic language, as if pared down austerely to fundamental elements, is still that of a poet whose ear remains attuned to the internal *difrasismo* of words, to their internal dislocations and doublings in both sound and sense: the pun on ripping and weeping in tears; the hesitation as to whether cross, in this one of many usages throughout, is to be taken as the crucifix or—as it then becomes—an adjectival noun; the uncertainty as to whether "sponge" is to be taken literally, and then as an allusion to the vinegar-sopped sponge offered to Christ in his agony on the cross, or as a metaphor for "spongy tissue." The uncertainty means that at every moment we must be unsure as to whether we are reading here a medical or a religious language.

Even in its final, gentle prose stanza, the poem's language retains its alertness to the path along which, in this prose that is at once supple and branching, it continually feels its way forward:

> What else but that bright element of home yellow consists like unbroken surface, like so much that was not, not the jagged night, its rupture nor

spill? Unimpeded chrome as if a gain the issue in spires were noon and first illumination at once one. O bright home this course again a gain of course.

In these last words, both of the poem and of his final volume, Arteaga seems to condense the signature phrases of two great European modernists, T. S. Eliot's "In my end is my beginning" and Samuel Beckett's "you must go on, I can't go on, I will go on."[21] But it is with his own characteristic, word-dividing signature that he signs off, with the cross of a chiasmus, X. Though Arteaga died prematurely, before that new poetic course could fully be laid down, *Act Zero* stands as a fitting coda to the work, an unwittingly final volume that still opens to the new directions towards which his singular Xicanx poetics continues to point the way.

NOTES

1. From Arteaga's epigraph to the book *Cantos*. Throughout this introduction, I am following his example in using the spelling Xicanx where reader's might expect Chicano, Chicana, and/or Chicanx. I have no doubt that Arteaga would have embraced a usage that became widely current only after his death, though always in the spirit of playfulness and variability that this epigraph signals, rather than as a sign of identity. For some cautions about the "easy embrace of the X" and "what it crosses out or eliminates from consideration when we traffic in contemporary identity politics," see Richard T. Rodríguez, "X Marks the Spot," *Cultural Dynamics* 29.3 (2017), 203 and passim, 202–13.

2. The comment was in a letter from Gilles Deleuze to Alfred Arteaga, 10/12/1991: "vous faites partie de ces rares poètes qui savent dresser ou tailler dans leur langue une nouvelle langue."

3. See Arteaga, "Late Epic, Post Postmodern," the final chapter of *Chicano Poetics: Heterotexts and Hybridities* (Cambridge: Cambridge University Press, 1997), 155.

4. Arteaga discusses at length Villagrá's poem as a belated epic form in "Late Epic, Post Postmodern," pp. 126–55.

5. See Jean-Luc Nancy, "Cut Throat Sun," in Alfred Arteaga, *An Other Tongue* (Durham, NC: Duke University Press, 1994), 113–23. Arteaga later cites Nancy's essay in emphasizing that for the Chicano subject, *mestizaje* is not a state or a thing, but a condition that is "unfinalized" and "still becoming." See Arteaga, "Beasts and Jagged Strokes of Color," in *Chicano Poetics*, 100.

6. On the figure of the chiasmus, see Arteaga, "Tricks of Gender X-ing" in *Chicano Poetics*, 48.

7. See Arteaga, "An Other Tongue," in *Chicano Poetics*, 74.

8. Arteaga, "An Other Tongue," 73–74.

9. See Arteaga's discussion of Montoya's "El Louie" in "An Other Tongue," 70. At the same time, he offers an example of a "caló-ization" of poetic language in José Antonio Burciaga's "Poema en tres idiomas y caló," where Burciaga forms hybrids between both English and Spanish and Spanish and Nahuatl, e.g., *locotl*, *loco* + *-tl*, crazy.

10. Since the verb *se taire*, to be silent, derives from Latin *tacere*, root also of English *tacit*, the implied echo is quite plausible. For Sor Juana's own multilingual poetic compositions and on her *Respuesta*, see Arteaga, "Tricks of Gender X-ing," in *Chicano Poetics*, 44–65.

11. See, for example, not only other poems in this particular volume, like the elaborate aural "translation" of the poem "muñeca, muñequita" into the facing "world-echo, little world-echo," but in such poems as "Net Laguna" in *Red* or "Sin Control" and "En lugar de la nada" in *Act Zero*.

12. Arteaga, "Mestizaje/Difrasismo," in *Chicano Poetics*, 6.

13. See Miguel León-Portilla, *Fifteen Poets of the Aztec World* (Norman, OK: University of Oklahoma Press, 1992), 48. Also, Angel María Garibay, *Llave del Náhuatl* (Mexico: Porrua, 1970), 117; cited by Arteaga, "Mestizaje/Difrasismo," 157n.

14. On the use of red and black inks in Meso-American scripts, see León-Portilla, *Fifteen Poets*, 15–16. Arteaga may also have in mind Ezra Pound's famous citation of Ernest Fenollosa's work on the Chinese ideogram, in which he uses the example of the ideogram for red that is a composite of "the abbreviated pictures for ROSE CHERRY IRON RUST FLAMINGO." See Ezra Pound, *ABC of Reading* (London: Faber and Faber, 1951), 22.

15. For Bakhtin's terms, see M. M. Bakhtin, *The Dialogic Imagination: Four Essays*, ed. Michael Holquist, trans. Caryl Emerson and Michael Holquist (Austin, TX: University of Texas Press, 1981), 425–26.

16. Arteaga, "Mestizaje/Difrasismo," in *Chicano Poetics*, 15.

17. For Nezahualcoyotl's life and surviving poems, including "Song of the Flight," see León-Portilla, *Fifteen Poets*, 70–98.

18. See Marie Uguay, *L'outre-vie* (Montréal: Éditons du Noroît, 1979). Jean-Claude Labrecque documented her life and work in his film *Marie Uguay: Portrait Intime* (1982). Uguay is also alluded to in *Love in the Time of Aftershocks*, VII.

19. On Nezahualcoyotl's belief that "Tloqueh Nahuaqueh was "the Giver of Life in whose book of paintings we exist," see León-Portilla, *Fifteen Poets*, 80–88.

20. Jacques Derrida, *The Other Heading: Reflections on Today's Europe*, trans. Pascale-Anne Brault and Michael B. Naas (Bloomington: Indiana University Press, 1992), 24.

21. See T. S. Eliot, "East Coker V," in *Four Quartets*, in *Collected Poems, 1909–1962* (London: Faber and Faber, 1968), 204; and Samuel Beckett, *The Unnamable*, in *Molloy, Malone Dies, The Unnamable* (London: Calder and Boyars, 1973), 418.

EDITOR'S ACKNOWLEDGMENTS

This collection is, above all, an act of recognition and of gratitude to Alfred Arteaga. Beyond the sensuous intelligence of his poetry that so richly rewards reading and rereading, his friendship and his wry wisdom were a privilege to enjoy over many years. The afterlife of these poems is also the gift of a companionship too abruptly cut off. This book is dedicated to all those in whose company Alfred so unreservedly delighted.

My thanks to the Arteaga family, and in particular to his daughters, Marisol, Xóchitl, and Mireya, for so generously allowing me to edit this volume and for kindly giving me so much help and access to everything from documents and recordings to memories and encouragement. As he did so many times before, Alfred would have prefaced this book "para mis hijas."

I am grateful to Gronk for so readily allowing the reproduction of his painting "The Man without Desire" as the cover of this book, and to Chon Noriega and the Chicano Studies Research Center at the University of California, Los Angeles for supplying the image. And to Trevor Joyce for the author photograph.

Cherríe Moraga's foreword speaks for itself, and my thanks are due not only for her deep appreciation of Alfred's work, but also for her own life's work, which he so admired. No words of mine could put things as well as he once did: "she speaks differently, therefore things are different."

My thanks to Diana Echeverría, without whose research assistance, speedy work, and great good humor at the initial stage of this project, these texts might never have come together. Thanks to Fred Moten, for opening the door. To Suzanna Tamminen, who has been so patient and supportive an editor throughout the process of pulling this collection together; and to Jim Schley, whose attentive copyediting—at once careful and caring—has ensured this text's fidelity to its author. To Ricky Rodriguez, for the details and the memories. To Carolina González, not only for sharing the original *Cartas* but also for illuminating Alfred's irrepressibly dialogical way of working. To Sarita See, as ever, for sustaining me through what has been at once a labor of love and of mourning.

cantos

X antecanto: the xicano sign

These cantos chicanos begin with X and end with X. They are examples of xicano verse, verse marked with the cross, the border cross of alambre y río, the cross of Jesus X in Native America, the nahuatl X in méxico, mexicano, xicano. It is our mark, our cross, our X, our sign never ceasing being born at the point of two arrows colliding, X, and at the gentle laying of one line over another line, X. It is the sound we make to mark one and other, August 29, familia, raza, as well as to exclude ourselves from the patterns of death imposed from without. We sign the X each time we speak we cross at least one border. And because it is our sign andamos cruzando cruzados, naciendo siendo xicanos otra vez, cada vez, esta vez. I am the point of my own X but the arms, los brazos vienen de lejos, and the arms reach far.

Nacido, East Los X3; Escribo, San Jo X4: AA

CANTOS PRIMEROS

PRIMERO

Arrival

First, the island.
The cross of truth.
Another island.
A continent.
A line, half water, half metal.

An island of birds, "Ccollanan."
An island of birds,
"Ccollanan Pachacutec!"
Sounds above an island, in
the air, trees, "Ccollanan Pachacutec!"
Female sounds. "Ricuy
anceacunac yahuarniy richacaucuta!"
An island of female birds, imagine
the sounds, the air, the trees, at times
the silence, the slither in thorns.

So perfect a shape, right
angles, the globe yields to so
straight a line, look. One
line, zenith to nadir, heaven,
precipitation. The only other,
straighter still than the horizon
we see at sea, perfect: paradise.
That horizontal line, from
old to new, he knew would yield,
yes, so perfect a move, he
knew, yes, so perfect a shape
yes.

Trees caught his thoughts.
Birds and onshores brought them
from the boats. She knew those
thoughts, heard those songs.
Could there be one more island?
Birds, sounds, perhaps pearls,
gold? Eden-Guanahaní, perhaps
another? "O my Marina, my new
found island. License my roaving
hands, and let them go, before,
behind, between, above, below."
West.

América, América. Feminine
first name, continent named
for him. América.
Here, Santa Fe. Here, the true
faith. I claim in the name of
the father. Land of thorns,
in the name of the son.

The edge of this world
and the other, is marked
in water: ocean, river, wave to
her, she waits on the other
side. Aquí, se llama la Juana,
de apellido Juárez, india,
prieta y chaparra, la que le encanta
al gringo, al gachupín.

Island of cactus, genus
Cuauhtémoc. Island of rose,
land of thorns. Pedro de
Alvarado, an eagle, la
región transparente, a
night of smoke. Marina
Nightear, an ocean contained
in one woman, as it was in
the beginning, world
without end, fallen
eagle.

So feminine a shape. So female
a bay. Another shape: gliding
birds. Another: touching trees.
True name of woman, Vera Cruz,
body of woman. "He named me
Xochitepec, yes so we are all flowers
of the mountain, all a woman's body,
that was one true thing he said in
his life." Above, birds,
leaves, above so woman a form.
Las quince letras: not the seven words:
Contestó Malintzin, "yes
I said yes I will Yes."

En el nombre
de la Virgen de las Espinas,
ella que en buen ora nasco,
this archeology is born: here
tibia, here ball courts, codices,
teeth. Inside, the caves are
painted. Here an architecture,
see, toco, toco,
tocotín:

Tla ya timohuica,
totlazo Zuapilli,
maca ammo, Tonantzin,
titechemoilcahuíliz.
Mati itlatol ihiyo
Huel ni machicáhuac
no teco qui mati.

En la sangre, en las espinas
de la Virgen de Santa Fe,
these names are written:
América Estados-Unidos, née
México. I name her
Flower of the Mountain,
Coatepec-Cihuatepec-Cuicatepec
Amor Silvestre,
Terra Nova,
Cuerpo de Mujer.

The edge of this world
and the other, is marked
in metal: on this side America,
on this side América.
Nights they spill from
San Diego and Los Angeles
threading the steel mesh
como nada, los verdaderos
alambristas, buscando el cuerpo
de mujer, buscando,
Xochitepec.

SEGUNDO

Textos vivos

En lo negro that is blackness,
en lo negro, that negritude,
in that night sheet sin
cloud sin moon sky, en lo negro, cielo
vivo
in that black sheet stretched
from one hand a un autre
este negro ósculo
oscuro de papel manantial
de mano a mano que ves
esta vez, Je est,
yes, in that yes blank sin
blanco, black held in your now
hand hear hand, aquí, mano vocal,
you see yes, que ves esta vez, negro
vivo
que ves, que lees, el negro que lees,
ahora que lees, aquí que lees
en el negro que lees, ahora y aquí
que lees el pecado sin negro
vivo

Entre las manos extiendes la red
from one hand to the other que lees,
desde una mano, one to another,
la red extiende, hoja colorada no
suelta, la red extendida y colorada
from one hand to the other que ves,
l'outre-vie du texte, outre-texte,
que lees, la red que detienes
al momento, that you read
entre estas dos manos
vivas

aquel color del filo, aquellas
marcas también, that you
hold from one hand tú que
ves, tú who reads this instant,
that color del filo there you
see, know you see there red, sí you
read en aquellas rojas marcas
vivas
extended red, color of solstice
that moment only, red solo, red
color that instant, manos escritas,
extendiendo lo rojo, red color of
manuscript soltice,
tú, tú que lees el estreno
nuevamente rojo, this only soltice,
rojoglífico, color that you read,
from hand, tu mano a esa obra,
rojo you read, aqui, enfrente las
hojas estrechas, no sueltas,
vivas

Here it is, the equinox, next to
the hand's skin, beside the other's
too, que ves desocupado
lector, inexplicablemente
despierto, la red negra, la hoja roja:
the black that is silence, letter,
the red that is on, syllable,
negroglífico, rojezcrito, here
it is lying between your hands
alive red alive black, here
it is next to and beside lies
alife

Negrita, Red Man,
de isla y continente
brilliant skins, bright red,
bright black:
hope, splendor, mirror.
Ella, la California, es la serga
de Esplandián, hija
ilegítima de la amada de jaula.
Y él, el bravo Californio, niño perdido,
nuevamente salido y producido,
de aquellas vivas llamas y cenizas,
del ardentísimo y Christianísimo Filipo
que pues en Nueva México quiso ver fénix.

Terra Nova:
hope, splendor, mirror. Bright
back, reflecting, tezcatl,
reflect, nechichauallano,
mirror: A new island of pearls
in the black hands of women; a new
continent of men blood colored::

tlilli in quecholli
tlilli in tlapalli
in ixochiuh in xronotopxopan
xiuhtlacuilolli ya amoxcalitec
krugozory:
xicancuicatl

TERCERO

El viaje

White, from white Mictlan, south,
to Xopan, to Tenochtitlan,
"Nosotros descendimos hasta
el río impasible, nosotros de piel
roja, buscando la señal: una isla
en las montañas, en las nubes
claras de águilas, la serpiente
despeñada, el nopal antípoda.
A una isla mixtitlan, a la isla mixtitlan,
dimos el nombre
Isla Xochitepec."
From Aztlan, the word made motion,
tentli, yollotl, yolotia,
to eagle, to snake, to cactus,
each black.

Old man, conquistador,
Bavieca, Tizón and Colada,
father of Coyote, Chamizo,
Sambaigo and Combujo,
father of Lobo, of Barquino,
of Mulato, father of Mestizo.
"From Europe's cold black waters
to Tepeyac, Flower of the Mountain,
where sad children shall kneel
before us. In the name of Our Lady
of the Thorns, we shall baptize a
Juan-Diego Oxomoco, a Marina Nightear,
baptize a María Castellano Cortés,
a Rodrigo Río-Bravo."
And west, dark
women and pearls. "Esplandián!
Plus Ultra, Esplandián!"

Old words made blood,
old words made
new.

Many mothers, a father who
loosed dogs one sad night,
feathers from the quetzal, a
bird who now coos in Spanish.
From the high plateau, from a
gulf town, across desert to one
river, half water, half metal. A
mesh of steel and spray, only
threaded by the mad. Railroads
to the madness, highways to the
cities of the mad, and a boat.
"J'ai rêvé le fleuve m'a laissé
descendre où je voulais." In
my dream, a woman approaches
the fence, she offers mezcal,
there is something
dead in the liquid, we
drink from the common bottle,
our skins are the same
color, in the darkness
agave and mesquite
seem one.

Lone star, bear flag,
Fredonia.
Sea to shining ore.
To San Antonio, Santa Fe,
Monterey. To Tijuana or Juarez
Saturday night, border
Chapultepec: young girls
descend, unfurl to drunken
gringos, las heroicas, "Viva
el pinche dólar." Chapultepec,
grasshopper hill: a park

devoted to the pleasure of
marines, devoted to
grasshoppers. Three brown
girls of age stroll by, their color
flagrant.
Long live the land
of plenty.

"If I could fly from this
island of clouds, from this
green island of clouds, from
this green island of orange
men lions, not follow
for long months, like cattle or
breaking sea on reef.
All exiles are kings' sons, after all.
Sad Tara. Leaden sea. Bright heavens."
To Canada, America, Churubusco,
Chapultepec. Flight of John Riley.
Harp of Erin, a Shamrock, a green field.
Was it Col. Bennet Riley or was
it Capt. O'Shay? 16 hanged at
San Angel, April 9, 1847. 4 hanged
at Mixcoac, April 10. 30 hanged
at Chapultepec, grasshopper hill,
where the children heroes took
flight, April 13. The rest: 50 lashes,
an iron collar with 3 prongs, 6
inches, 8 pounds each; a head shaving;
a D branded on the cheek.
From green Tara island to
green Tenochtitlan island,
from Erin to Aztlan,
I remember,
then.

Primero, el poder y la palabra. Napoleón
o el poder del pasado, Juárez o
el poder de la raza. Entre las
dos orillas del poder, un puente:
Carlota, que convierte
la historia de ambos poderes
en teatro. Habla la Hapsburg,
"J'aurais voulu montrer aux
enfants ces dorades, ces serpents
emplumés, cette pyramide. Les
mexicains ont bercé mes détrades,
et d'ineffables ventes m'ont ailée
par instants. Ce pays sauvage,
ce bateau perdu."
Encore

QUARTO

Xronotop Xicano

Aguila negra, rojo chante.
Tinta y pluma.
Textos vivos,
written people: the vato
with la vida loca on his neck,
the vata with p.v., the ganga with
tears, the shining cross. Varrio
walls: codices; storefront
placazos: varrio names,
desafíos, people names.
Written cars, names etched
in glass, "Land of a Thousand
Dances." Placas
and love etched in schools.

Faces of Indians branded
by Spaniards.
Faces of Irishmen branded
by Americans.
Gachupín: he who kicks
with the boot.
Yankee: new man, of the
new world, Yancuic.
Xicano: cantador, namer.

xicancuicatl
floricanto
canto
canto

Santa Cruz, 1986

OLD FORMS NEW

5 *Romance Blanco*

There is the man who comes to the door, to
the nine year old girl, "I," does not know him.
No, "No," he puts his foot to the door, kicks,
Her eye, her hand, her nine year leg too waits.
He claims he wants to eat food, "I am nine,
but can talk to a man whose foot breaks here:
the door is mine." This wall, the whole house too.
No one here will give you food. Nor will I.

His boots come from Spain. He has the steel of
his trade at his side. Eyes stare, but no tongue
speaks, "No," or "Sí." A nine year old girl stands
still, "I can speak 'No' for man, for him whose
name claims me, 'No' for the one I come from
but can't talk to you man whose foot breaks now.
The voice is mine." This word, the whole word too.
He leaves. Old, dust, smoke-blood, empty dead time.

6 *Corrido Blanco*

Her notebook declares, "If for you fathers
my logos suffers too, (what did Paul say?)
'Mulieres' You 'in Ecclesia tace-
ant.' Too, mujeres en iglesia, you

te nacen, palabrita, tú, mia."
In the schools from Rome, you are born living,
from London too: nace la palabra.
And you become and kill a tongue or two.

Criolla, woman whose word I see, hear,
maestra, teacher, eye and ear and tongue
for me. Here I am one nine year old boy.
No hay razón, sólo poder. Here I

hear, see, palabra suya, "Know: children
be silent in school. No language, or word
or sound you know from homelands. Ameri-
ca, no way to spell it but one. I know."

Houston–Santa Cruz, 1988

CANTOS EUROPEOS

7 *NW6*

How many degrees whiter
north? How dead into the
dead land: Mictlan:
white, north, far land,
in the quiet and still white
whisper of faint death?
Northern, northern land.

Yet what is the color that transforms words
and names from breathing beasts and human
beings with arms and blood and children too?

What does Tupac Amarú say, does
Cuauhtémoc say, does
Lolita Lebrón have to say?

"Green island,
'Black Island.'"
Broken in(to) lands, bones in
black & white X-rays.

And if the northern northern land were
not so edged in bleak seas nor so
alone, the sad birds did not freeze
in cavern streets and break like stone
in rare shade, what then? Would

it collect the voice of the dead in
choir and give rein to chant so
lonely and keen a wail, that it could
make me forget?
Or remember that in the land of
the dead, the dead breed faster than we
can guess, having sex by memory, more
than we can do?

Oh Mictlan, northern land,
white one death,
band and hue of time stretched thin,
what then?

8 *muñeca, muñequita*

muñeca de paja
muñequita
hecha de paja
muñequita
no tienes nada
muñequita
nomás la paja
muñequita

qué vas a ser
cuando crezcas
en el verano
de año que entra
mamá o
muchachita
o quedas paja
muñequita

8 *world-echo, little world-echo*

world-echo on the page
little world-echo
ambiguous page
little world-echo
no tender nothing
little world-echo
names on the page
little world-echo

why was a lord
wandering crazy
in the veranda
but did not enter
mother of
so much and so little
on the dearest page
little world-echo

9 *The Small Sea of Europe*

At the end of the eighteenth century, Hindu law,
insofar as it can be described as a unitary system, operated
in terms of four texts that "staged" a four-part episteme defined
by the subject's use of memory: *sruti* (the heard), *smriti*
(the remembered), *sastra* (the learned-from-another),
and *vyavahara* (the performed-in-exchange).
Gayatri Chakravorty Spivak

In Europe's small sea,
a system of exchange:
forms of life
and motion in sign.

The Case in Point-

Verkehr:
'the motion of women, of slaves,
in sleekcongested automobiles, trunks
with drugs'

Verkehr,
from the Sanscrit, (small sea),
vyavahara:
'performance traffic,
former act of transformation,
an exchange.'
Ecos escritos: *Sruti*, *Smriti*, *Sastra*
three sisters in myth, very
sources of Europe, Western Man,
the very sounds slipping: 3Ss, sans(é)crit
3Ss:
3Ss: ecos escritos (S grito)

Again, then.
Verkehr:
S_1 in the automobile beside S_2, S_3
at the wheel, 'Sister . . .' furtive, slave-like
movements (escape? from/to what/where?)
But who can drive? Of course, S_2 remembers,
tells, S_1 hears, inserts the key,
demonstrates, S_3 learns, starts the motor: of
course, escape, With-Drugs o wild & steering slave
through furtive traffic, changing lanes, exchanging
places of courses, escape:
Sruti hears, Smriti recalls, Sastra learns from an   other:
S drive and drive, verkehr
S *verkehr*: vyavahara
a performance, vyavahara,
the S sound of abandon.

(Or) Again:
Sastra (née 'furtive slave') learned
furtive from
Sruti: (née 'furtive slave') heard
furtive from
Smriti (née 'furtive slave') remembers
furtive from
the small sea of history, the big C of capital,
first squirt of legend, trancendental quill
and myth-inks, rib stain here first
no ear, no hearing, across which sheets first
defined smear.

I remember Smriti, in the dictionary,
Verkehr:
'fast women in cars escape with drugs'
like Texas, but this is Berlin
to Paris, night rides hard riding off course
3 woman Ss written off across this old sad continent
fast esses, stained-fast essences, the Ss senses (S sense)
of woman defi(l/n)ed.

Some big *Dichtung*
this place,
a ce.

London, 1988

10 *À mon seul désir*

5.2.89

La brisa, la frialdad
de aquel domingo en París,
día húmedo: yo recuerdo como
las meras piedras de la calle
murmuraban esas sílabas sibilantes
en tiempo con tus pies, mis pies
por el paseo antiguo de París
por la tarde.
Te veo todavía, tú, mujer
de otro tiempo, de visiones,
tú valoras los sentidos que todavía
actualizan esta tela vital. ¿Cuáles
animales franceses te revelan hoy
día y a la ánima perceptible ese día pasado, allí en París?
Había sonidos desvanecidos, ese domingo,
de un nivel más elevado que el de piedra,
más líquido y tenue: ya oigo y no oigo ya.
Si pudiéramos hablar, estuviéramos hablando,
en el momento actual, (pero, sí, ¿cuál momento, qué texto?)
¿que no nos pararíamos nosotros mismos,
y no oiríamos, una vez más, este sonido brutal
y el eco ajeno, dos rasgos tejidos
de la noche parisiense?
Y en fin, se nota tu boca presente
y el parto de las notas afines, ausente,
¿tu palabra, tal como tu sonido?
si parisílabos los
dos, parisílabos, sí

Oigo:

«Un miedo que tengo, de no sé qué, me persigue, me plasma, forma ambos emociones y modos, el miedo que es mi texto y el preámbulo mío. ¿Qué no? Yo no sé ni quién soy, ni para qué, para quién soy, ni estoy, esta tarde en París, día húmedo, día antiguo, perfectamente mío, día mío, París, vía antigua, avenida a la calle. Cómo me asustan estas huellas: el palimpsesto parisiense, esfumado, muy esfumado; la paleta diurnal y desteñida; la acuarela que pertenece al invierno débil y pálido; todos de la tarde perdida, la tela ajena y tejida. Y a veces me asusta el color de algo, tal sonido de tal animal, por ejemplo, la ausencia tuya o la humedad del paseo visto por mi parte, por el punto de vista mío. ¿Qué no me asusta? Así como digo yo, así, así me sigue, sin son, pero así. Y así yo recuerdo los animales que pintarrajaban ellos mismos en las piedras, digo paredes, de tal pueblo, no me acuerdo el nombre, ni cómo se llama ¿te acuerdas? sí, de seguro. ¿Cuántos pequeños rasgos contiguos a las veredas y vaderas antiguas? ¿Cuántas marcas, manchas y rastras persistentes? como te explico así. Quizás en la tarde de un día de invierno por ejemplo, oirás, entre los edificios antiguos de París por una tarde húmeda, día húmedo, como es, un eco tan desconocido, como te digo, que si fuera posible, nunca más dormirías.

«Ya sí, así, animal doloroso, rasgar y derramar para siempre hasta siempre, así, que sí. Yo recuerdo cuando (y antes que) oigo, porque nunca oigo sin recordar o haber recordado antes, aquella memoria, imagen y pánico, día doloroso como escribo yo, Pluma y Tinta: mi animal, animal mío, persigue, domingo mío, entre las ramblas antiguas de París, escritas por la tarde, día y agua, agua y animal, París mío.

«O animal claro de huella y presencia, cuerpo de agua de piedra de brisa, animal que asoma, con hebras rojas y negras y un azul tan profundo que debe significar, que me asombra, que me pasma a mí: Por mis calles de mi pueblo, de mi tiempo de mis aguas, por el tiempo, por lo bueno hasta siempre hasta siempre. O animal, por los míos, miedo y garra de la vida cotidiana: ¿qué y qué pues? ¿En qué forma? la próxima vez, esta vez, por mi tarde, París tan tarde. O pueblo mío, el susto precisa la mancha, el rasgo nunca aclara, ¿letra y humo significan todavía, hoy día? Día de agua. ¿Tú y yo? Cuáles animales se mueven por mis calles día tras día, tras día, y no imagino de la noche, París, pueblo antiguo, marea de susto, animal herido, animal mío, día de fiesta, día que se inmuta, día corto de invierno, débil, dominguito día 7.»

¿La tinta? ¿Dónde y cuándo quedará?
¿Nace en la luz, la paleta, la pluma,
o alrededor del órgano de la vista?
Literalmente no es una metáfora,
la franja y las hebras del ojo.
Pero ¿en qué consiste un color
que mete y sale, sometiéndose a
un orden solitario, distinto,
una tela imponiéndose entre
la piedra y el tacto húmedo? ¿Verde,
la franja tal como las hebras?
Es una dirección pura,
una trayectoria de huellas nomás;
es una locución hablada con
temor, vista por alguien.
Aquí la brisa anima
el discurso fabricado y el respiro brutal.
El pueblo de colores bajos y mates
se trasluce en tintas y hebras claras y matizadas.
El día de varios verdes
desborda la fábrica del eco
que eres y que quedas, tú, mujer, aquí
en tu antiguo París.
Fíjate.
El pájaro no es nada, un son gastado.
Los pies hacen el ruido, las trazas, la vista.
Tú asomas, tejes el sonido y el son
con la brisa y la frialdad del momento de mi,
digo, de nuestro domingo.

Una niña entra y sale una maravilla.
O mejor, se trazuma por la tela
que es París por la tarde,
una persona.
Milagro ¿qué no?

Paris, 1989

11 *Rocamador, Asleep*

What trains cross
the night childhood
each stop passing still.

Barcelona, 1989

AL PIE DE LA LETRA

12 *Letters of Color*

No existe el amanecer. No existe el atardecer.
El sol mismo ha muerto.
Sólo quedan las nubes. Absolutas. Verdes.
Juan Felipe Herrera

each
green eye in a heaven of blue, a fistfull
of understanding
Lorna Dee Cervantes

Verde no eres tú
Rosario Castellanos

"Green is most sad.
Germany is this color
and shines
this temperature
always . . ."
—she writes
me in letters. What
could she mean, these
words this breath, these
proofs of woman
to me?
The letters, of course, I know
are not her:
She is not the green. Yet,
because she writes,
I write too. This is true.

So
I collect green: a rain forest monkey
hides there in tree, I see it; that whale breathes
a cold and broken green, passes the
California point; one green follows the sad
goodbye before the same old sleep,
I get it; bland pages enfold my (for now
I lay claim) color; and the green
I find forged in cannon and fatigue;
these greens
I gather.

But I do not visit Germany, despite
the joy of aluminum for gold,
I can't. Can her letters contain this?
I hold now, this very instant, in
my own hands, the saddest color,
the most Germanic green. Things I
have gathered with my own hands, things
encased in green, essentially green and
things seemingly green to any eye,
I hold. And
because she breathes,
I breathe too. Or this I lie.

I understand primate refuge in trees,
understand migration again
and again past the whaling town
site of slaughter, offal still I'm sure.
I know all the German glyphs like
lines which crease my hands,
I know them.

Yet letters come to me in breath almost
still, she does not tell me more than sad.
I am left only with weapons,
stupidly useless this second. She
writes. I am left with hands full of dumb
color, hands of useless speech that says no
thing, less.
This woman who writes sad green
colors me painted bird
wings before my eyes.

I have made children, planted trees.
I have killed men. I write these words.
My hands are green, I don't know
what it means.

Coyoacán, el otoño gris

Querido Alfredo—

Triste, verde y alemán fue la letra desaparecida de mi nombre—ojo—te mando una última letra: ausente, la tehuana-mexicana; presente, el mexicano-chicano. Escríbeme en caló, escribo, en color.

—Frida

13 *Canto Pacífico*

From my house I can see the widest sea
Pacific blue-black, green, and slate.
White where it breaks rock and
sprays on breeze, and almost
true black at night in fog.
El mar pacífico, names in Spanish
in Panama, perhaps in English
too, Sea of Peace, peaceful pacific, the
ocean that could hold all other seas
in its bays and gulfs and streams alone.

Now,
from my wooden and landed house, above
the sandstone cliff, past the sand's
touch, I see the pacific ocean. It is my view,
my sound, at times my breath.
And I am drawn into the family
of pacific people, we share the widest sea, every
day we bare our feet, hurl hook and net,
light candles in the naves of our souls.
In morning ritual, we turn and reflect,
recognize one and other, pacific people.
From Santa Cruz, I extend my hand
south to Cabo San Lucas, and from there, a baker,
a young girl with worn shoes, a sailor who
spends his day wet with spray, people I have
yet to meet but whose words I know, in turn,
they extend their hands, old and worn
and new, to farther hands
along the coast.
This ocean rite is not known to others but pacific people.
I share it now with you land locked ones,
and you whose seas are smaller, more silent, numb.
Perhaps you'll come one day to taste
pacific salt and someone will touch
your hand with his, with hers,
with mine.

Then
the peace in spray and wave,
the crashing surf and storm, can touch
your pacific hand. Then, the wildest storm,
the ocean's most wild dance against
the sandstone cliffs of Santa Cruz, the wave's
brave pass, silent over the deep abyss
off Cabo San Lucas, will seem nothing,
nothing like the sparks of torture in pacific Chile,
hand cuffed to metal bed frames, shot with electricity;
nothing like that moment Victor Jara
is cut off from language, cut off
from his pacific hands too.
The biggest wave,
blue-black, green or slate, that rips
through kelp forest, tide pool, and wide
sand bar, that swells above your
head, that curls and crushes and makes
everything confusion, that wave
is nothing like one desaparecido,
in pacific Guatemala;
nothing at all like the wall
of desperate cries, desperate sleepless
nights, and desperate madness
that swells above, rips through, and crushes
wife, brother, lover, of the one disappeared,
nothing at all.
Not the degree of cold surf, in January or
August winter, that makes each bare
foot bone cry out and panic; not the
retreating wave, the riptide back
and out, that could, if it so desired,
take with it to its watery home, a house
of stone; and not the rising tide
that cuts off the cove's retreat, imagine
the fear this creates at night, no not even this;
is nothing, nothing at all
like one dollar's worth of bullet,
boot, or contra's bandage,
not one.

O Pacific ocean, océano pacífico,
at this moment, I leave poetry. I watch
your motion from my window, and scan
ceaseless lines of waves coming in, coming
in relentless peace.
Who thinks of me, this moment,
thinking of the sea? Peaceful
Pacific Ocean, not at all not peaceful.
I see, hear, now I breathe, breaking
now, peaceful lines of waves,
breaking lines
of peaceful waves.

Santa Cruz, 1990

14 *Respuesta a Frida*

11/1, X4

On n'est pas morte mais déjà presque vivante, presque née, en train de naître peut-être, dans ce passage hors frontière et hors temps qui caractérise le désir. Désir de l'autre, désir du monde. . . . Traverser l'opacité du silence et inventer nos existences, nos amours, là où il n'y a plus de fatalité d'aucune sorte.
Marie Uguay

Q.F.—

[*cctbc*, Frida,
y *ccsa* letra *tdg* a
kiss, a lacuna. Each
drop of letter, yes, is
a fall of sorts.

Socc. So cae cada
gota, some heaven
missed.

2 color: Frieda *2* Frida,
I write *2u* Frida las *2*, *at*,
cuata *d2* misma cuata,
cuerpo *d2* mismo cuerpo,
F-Kerida, ambas
Frida, la misma *d2*
misma, Frieda.
at, 1 última respuesta:
en la cuna de las letras vacías,
echo el son hueco de un huerco,
y tras la arena de tierra y tiempo,
se suelta tu eco]

I am sorry such time has passed since you dropped me off that last letter. It is fall still in California and so much frigid earth between us (el otoño gris, Frida, California fría). I close my eyes as I write now (te rías). I can see your brown eyes, your brow, your row of black braids, (*O yes you're you, yet your own image becomes mine in my mind's eye, becomes our own in the blank of the letter o yes*) and black snakes curve above your head.

—AA

[Cuento
1 pierna, 1 ceja, 1 nacimiento,
2 Fridas, 3 ojos, unos picotazos, más sangre.
Menos 1 letra
(verde, el kalor alemán de Frieda la judía)
menos 1 letra
(trieste, la de una narrativa del único dolor posible
de andar quebrada en mala hora).
Encuentro
Frida menos la letra,
Frida, con una sola ceja, el plumado européo,
Frida la cuata tehuana, la cojita,
Frida menos la letra.]

P.S.—

"Se van como pájaros, de volada, like clumps of cut hair, each strand and bird signifying great love." Como cartas a los muertos and the soft clothing, buti suave, of the loved one. And the sobres amarillos, llenos de cartas llenas de letras de los desparecidos, such yellow butterflies in the air about me como las últimas letras de sexo, como s.

[la cuna vacía, sin son, sin *bb*,
2 las 2, parecidas, *2d* la letra
desaparecida, Frida, en fin,
d parte *d* mí, *atnlD.F.*, *Q.F.*, desde
X4 today, this last letter, I write
"*Q.F.*," florecida en caló. 2 flor yo canto,
color de caló:
trieste, colorado, y de aztlán.]

Y en fin, F,
¿quién más falta la letra?
¿la poeta que ahora canta en caló, o
el pintor que miró un color
encarnado por los límites de todos los
ayeres, o
la lectora que apretará en las manos,
al acabar de leer, una vida literalmente
vaciada?

Just as,
venadita,
the eighteen letters = las quince letras,
we come *bbn*
la cuna of the letter.

San José–Chicago, 1990

15 *For My Lady Going to War*

It is true
man and all his stories
fill our speaking mouths with words,
sand so dry we can never spit it all out.
Our dreaming skulls cannot keep out
the constant pricking of old tales
but crack and break instead.
Our shadows are black
and thicken because so many
others have crossed this way before.
This is all too true.

But I swear
when our two bodies touch,
when my flesh and your flesh
wage the dance making life, the
gasp and grab like death,
there in the light of what we two do,
I am
one man
and I imagine you
one woman.

Berkeley, 1991

“el Mundo iluminado, y yo despierta.”
SJ de la X

house with the blue bed

Blood, Sand, Blood

for kyf

A perfect walk up from the water
round Mullaghmore, the little boats
becoming more so, shrink
in view then wait in memory
behind the hill. Tomorrow Bundoran
or Lissadell, it makes such little difference,
we'll walk about the same, and this
bright light can neither repeat nor fade.
Though pleasure craft may diminish and finally
sink from view, though I sweat, you slow,
we are the distant sinking's fiery glow.

1 *sand*

There is no sand like this anywhere else. The steps themselves lose themselves at each step, not the trace, for I sink nearly to my knee at each step and leave a trail of deep tracks, but the trajectory of step is lost in the act of each puncture I make in such sand. What is lost and what remains, or perhaps the better question I raise remembering walking there beside the North Atlantic has nothing to do with recalling the original action, but is simply, what do I make now as memory of something lost?

It is summer sand, summer on Donegal Bay, or Bá Dhún na nGall, as it is untranslated in the Irish, halfway and walking distance between Streedagh and Mullaghmore. Streedagh is where ships lost from the Armada washed up, where Spaniards were eaten by the Irish, as the locals like to say. Mullaghmore is where Mountbatten was killed by an IRA blast. The sand has a consistency something like cake frosting that has been allowed to sit: its surface is smooth, stiff, almost hard but extremely thin. The pressure of any human foot breaks through to the most loosely packed, aerated interior. Each step forgets its forward trajectory and succumbs to a flash of panic that comes from the strength and very weakness of the step. Our feet walk not so much confidently as they do relatively ignorant, disinterested in our trail of steps yet jerked to reaction at the trip, stub, twist, or sudden plunge.

It is sand like no other I've encountered I am sure. The broad beach peels back from the Bay and North Atlantic across from Dernish, the tiny island where Dermot wanted to buy one of the two houses but settled instead on Loughaun, the eroding point, which is gradually becoming island. Facing the open bay and sea beyond, the beach is sharp in its rise from the water, the sand, a steep angle for a couple of meters before it flattens out in the wide beach. It is a warm sand, the summer of the decade, it had been declared over and again, yet the water cooler there than at Streedagh or Lissadell or Rosses Point.

That sand deceives by a firmness, its surface, that belies a soft interior. It is a broad beach between two points of violent history just minutes in Co Sligo from Counties Leitrim and Donegal and from Co Fermanagh, the westernmost of Northern Ireland. It is a firm surface of memory, steps across a sand between the Irish Republic and the United Kingdom, deceiving in its appearance and first tentative touch. No one can walk its skin, any human foot would break through, and at each breaking, a sense of direction is lost, the purpose of the step shaken off in the surprise of the break. The skin is warmer than the interior beneath; it is the reverse of the human body, than the skin and blood of the foot, for example. I recall walking there, losing steps there, as in no other place. In truth I lost my way coming aware of each single step.

The sand on Galveston is very fine. I have spent almost as much time walking that beach on the Gulf of Mexico as I have spent stepping into the Irish beach halfway between Streedagh and Mullaghmore, that is, very little time. Galveston is flatter than Ireland, and if it weren't that it is surrounded by water, I imagine I could smack a cue ball on Galveston grass and knock an eight ball into a corner pocket in Houston. On the gulf side, tiny ripples break, imitate waves, with crests of moss-colored foam, colored by the film of free petroleum. The sand itself approaches powder and could rightly be called so were it not for the humidity.

But the Galveston sand itself means next to nothing to me. It is a sand of little consequence that occurs to me after considering a walk in Co Sligo, each step as deep as it was forward. Then, I pause, what is it of Galveston that asserts its presence before my mind's eye, memory and heart, what that asserts presence after recalling that Irish beach? There is the link, sand to sand, beach to beach, clearly, an echo, mirror or repetition of course, but just as soon and as likely, it is a step not taken: Galveston fades from my memory, pale as an afterthought, as soon as presence, a potential here for consideration, manifests, the sands of Galveston fade or are rejected or perhaps even, are aborted before proper formation.

There are as many other images that could arise after the Irish steps other than the Texan sky as there are stars yet unseen in the night sky. Why the Gulf of Mexico after the North Atlantic? Why indeed. Why not instead, or even now replacing the vision of Galveston sands, the impossibility of movement on the Angel tube platform or fleeing tear gas and the police off Whittier Boulevard or the letter never posted to Megève? *What*, I say is a primary question of human thought, and I ask, *what is next?* And in parallel I wonder, *what instead?* Or simply, *what not?*

As such I am as easily again at the Irish seashore considering once again a sand I have never conceived before. With the write of the poet, seeing a sand once again that I have never seen before. It is a sand of most fragile surface; it skirts the lip of the ocean, and it is profound. My tracks behind me mark a clear path to my present site and state, of this I have little doubt. Before me an unbroken plane of surface, sand I could track across, in posse, and in esse in my imagination and space and time. I stand up to my knees in sand; I cannot see my feet, cool below the fragile surface somewhere below, somehow oddly not present. They are not on the plane of my tracks, on the plane of the surface of the warm and easily ruptured sand beside the North Atlantic on a hot summer, Irish day. What track, what step in the sand, next? What rupture of surface, what depth instead?

This is then what occurs to me next, now at this juncture, instead of a repetition of walks and beaches north and south: *what next? what instead?* I have begun this literal excursion with a simple walk in Ireland, and its presence as starting point forever colors what becomes present here after it and more particularly what what comes to be. Rather, at this moment, than follow the path across the sand or from sand to other sand, and even rather than consider what lies beneath the surface plane, that is, rather than direction and alternation, than linear movement and selective identification, than horizontal and vertical, rather than these, the matter of *rather* itself. Each step forward breaks a surface to some other. The Irish sand of fragile surface and profound depth is the point I begin again and again, both as a first time and as subsequent motion on a prescribed path. This is where I begin now, once again, present in the present, about to step and about to redefine my path. I begin then with a walk across Irish sand on a hot summer day. I begin not with the material matter there, but with the steps and the possibility of sand.

3 *air*

So what if the better part of a year has passed this rainy day late spring in Berkeley and as I look out it is toward the bay and the pacific beyond, which I cannot see for the dense gray fog, but that I believe is there? What does it mean to write and to conceive now and here, obscured from the sea, its cold water, its dark sand, once again my steps across a fragile surface? Is it a plain break in logic, a lie, or perhaps a falling from the span and order of time? Or is it merely the play of language set in motion by a lyric sensibility?

Straight inland from the beach, at the distance of a long walk (for what isn't walking distance in Ireland?), juts up from the brown plane of bog, green hay field, and slate-blue lough Ben Bulben, the broad, flat mountain that is the center of local reckoning and most commanding of landmarks in Yeats's country. I found myself at the foot of Ben Bulben late, late one night, some days after the St. John's Eve fires of Sligo and Donegal, and yet other days before the death of the young boy felled by a tractor in Ballyconnell. It was after midnight, heading toward 3 a.m., and the sky was full of deep red folds and reddish violet and cold deep blue; such a wonder, something never seen by me or by any of my ancestors, native as we are to Mesoamerica and Iberia, too far south to witness such a night sky. We were a small group, five in all: the kind poet who had just gotten money from the organization with stars on a blue field to write a screenplay in Irish; her son, the composer, a modern who wrote atonal; the hotel manager, at whose house we found ourselves, whose American wife had gone off for days, with a woman we imagined; the lost piano teacher, the only one that night I couldn't take my mind off; and five, me.

The land in from the sea to Ben Bulben is level, not flat, but level. There is variation, such as bogs where who knows what might be interred, preserved; slight surface undulations called hills, fields and breaks in the fields called roads. There is nothing till Ben Bulben to stop the wind. It is the north North Atlantic after all, and air might as naturally emanate from the polar ice-cap or Ellesmere Island as it might from Galveston and the warming zone of the gulf stream, even midsummer. But regardless of the source, its point of origin and thus its definition, for winds after all are named for their compass point source, nothing so much as unsettles the flow of wind until it comes against the broad and flat-topped mountain.

The hotel manager was hurting, that's certain, but took us into his home, gave us wine, and disappeared to barbecue salmon outdoors beneath the northern sky palette coming on 3 a.m. The poet drank befitting an Irish poet and drank more. She loved her son, that was evident, and managed to remain just enough of a conversant so as to prevent the two musicians from falling out, from condescension on the one hand and resentment on the other. The composer spoke to me about the kind of music Lyn Hejinian's husband does in San Francisco, in a vocabulary and syntax largely unknown to me. In the end, his speaking for the avant garde put me off; I think he had spent too much time in England.

The piano teacher was lost, small, and, by Irish standards, brown. Both she and I were at the mercy of the car owners: kind poet and sad hotelier. We had wanted to spend time alone together before she went back to her husband and I to my daughters. So we exited the house out the American-style sliding glass doors, I think Stan Getz was on the machine, out into the brilliant night sky and a senseless wind.

This is the point of evoking this memory: that wind. Stepping out of that house should have been into black. As we faced out to the sea there were no artificial lights before us, but there was the northern night sky. It was cool, a cool night but not cold, and the air was full of the sea, unimpeded in its rush east, in its rush across the mostly liquid undulating surface of the North Atlantic, across the mostly solid undulations of Co Sligo up to this point, to the very point the lost, small, and brown piano teacher and I stood, at the foot of Ben Bulben.

The wind broke up: were it personified it could be felt to panic, dazed. It lost its clear trajectory, breaking up into synecdoches of wind, purposeless and wild at the collision with the mountain. We stood at this surprise, winds coming at us from every direction: our hair, her dress, blown back and forth consecutively and back and forth and every which way all at once. This is the point: standing there with my back to Ben Bulben, next to the lost piano teacher, facing the sea, at the break up of the invisible but real push from the sea, in the chaos of simultaneous and multiple impulse, there I was alive that moment and I am alive this moment yet these two moments do not equate. Standing there not taking a step I, in a small way like the mountains, made chaos, broke the flow of air from the sea in fragments like meaning.

4 *breath*

In a late second millennium consideration of meaning in verse, Charles Olson focused on the air of meaning and a machine of writing. The typewriter, it seems, in its uniform progression of letter, space, and punctuation, could accurately register the pace of the poet, the flow of phrase, the beat of breath. Today, at the transition from that millennium to the next, I compose music with the help of several electronic machines. The notes I play are written to the staff as I play them, but being as I am human, my sequencing software offers me the ability to overcome that. I simply accept its offer to quantize and my flesh and blood sense of rhythm is digitized, each note is precisely placed on a temporal grid, each approaching perfect duration.

The differences between Olson's typewriter and my synthesizer and sequencer don't interest me at this point, nor do the differences between poet's breath and musician's fingering. Instead I am interested in a similarity, in an underlying assumption of both, in a faith in the projection of meaning across time. In a fundamental sense, I think Olson's typed text and my musical score project a syntax, an order for reading that imagines or tries to represent a passage across time. Perhaps this is more evident in the music: the staff indicates pitch vertically and indicates tempo, the beat over time, horizontally. That is, music is written from left to right, in an order of notes that implies a succession of sounds across a span of time. To quantize that succession is to regularize intervals according to an accurate and electronic clock. Olson's typed text, in its uniform succession, its indications of letter, space, punctuation, the very syllables' voicing and inhaling and exhaling, implies a similar succession across time. Neither notes nor syllables are written all at once or in chaotic fashion; they peel off in order, in a sequence construed not only in order but in time. The uniformity of the typewriter and the quantizing of the sequencer function similarly; they regularize a pace of meaning (syllable or note) over a span of time, whether it is the human time of breaths or electronic time of seconds.

But lest the quantizing make the electronic music too machine like, the sequencer also offers the opportunity to humanize, that is, to introduce error in the fixing of beat to clock and so imitate the human, imprecise flow and ebb of beat and rest.

5 *bodies*

There are three instances of the human body at rest that seem to me moments when immobility forced a reconsideration of what it is to act human. The instances are three occurrences I witnessed, three moments of local crisis, scattered in disparate locales, drawn together here in my text one after the other in a reading of difference.

I was browsing in Waterstone's bookstore when I heard the sharp protest of an automobile straining to stop, a long shriek of brakes. I have lived urban enough not to react instantly and uncooly to the sudden, be it racial slur, or as in this case, a distant commotion on the street, so that by the time I did walk out, a crowd had already gathered on Earl's Court Road.

There in the street, neat against the English kerb, lay a woman in her own blood. She seemed calm, awake, and reminded me, perhaps because of her hair, of Ophelia in Millais's painting, even though she did not hold her arms outstretched but rather before her, hands clasped as if in prayer. But they were not in prayer but clasping the hand of a young man crouched beside her. He said nothing; she said nothing. It appeared as if they had been strangers just moments prior. Traffic was stopped; people gathered slowly.

In the middle of the street, from about twenty meters away, came a woman with Ophelia's shoe. What else was there to do? The young man clutching her hand gave the broken woman the most than any of us could, in silence and in touch and in confirmation that he would be for her what she could no longer be for herself. All that was left was to retrieve the shoe, and the woman's approach meant that even the trivial too would be taken care of; there was no need for Ophelia to move.

Some time after this, at the most a few months, I found myself in Paris, at the top of a seven-story walk-up, in a room whose windows looked out the mansard roof, trying to dial the telephone. The phone was broken in a most interesting and vexing sort of way: it would dial only reluctantly and then without sound. I did not hear the car this time but was called to the window by deep cries of pain.

There in the street stories below lay a woman writhing in a small clearing between the French cars. She lay writhing, on her elbows, shifting left then right. She wore blue jeans, one leg of which bent in an impossible angle. She cried loudly, deep, throaty, as if for cries she had sampled the roars from the lion house at the San Francisco Zoo.

Beside her was a taxi, the taxi that broke her walk on the avenue des Gobelins. The driver was a dark man, what goes for Arabe in Paris. A pale man emerged from another car, yelled at the driver and in a most French way, slapped him. The pale man must have needed to do something, driven as he was by the woman's inability to get up and by her growls in primal French.

Much later, perhaps two years, I was at home in San José and for no particular reason approached the front window. There in the street before my house were three Mexicans, two men and a boy, Mexicans rather than Chicanos I would say because of their dress, though they could well have been Texanos. One man stood with the slight sway of a drunk, his hand pulled by the boy in a gesture that was perhaps familiar to the son. On the pavement before them in a bright red shirt lay a very still, very dark man. The standing man called to the still one; the boy seemed anxious to act some good.

Suddenly a navy blue-and-white San José PD car pulled up, carrying in it two of the same uniformed types that would make my daughter kneel before them and hold a gun to her head just a short time in the future and just a few houses down the street. Instantly the drunk Mexican panicked and tried to walk away; the boy, less afraid, hesitated. The two policemen got out of the car, grabbed the drunk Mexican, handcuffed him, and pushed him into the back seat of the car. They said something to the boy I could not hear; he took off frightened.

It was only then that they turned to the fallen man. He remained face down, motionless. The police made no effort to examine the fallen man but handcuffed him immediately. They picked up the body by its hands and dragged it to the curb, face in the gutter, legs stretched at a right angle into the street. Having done that they got on the radio for the paramedics.

6 *rape*

Shortly after first becoming a father, I returned to Los Angeles from New York with new baby daughter and wife. It was about the time I turned 24, and the father/husband/family thing seemed yet new and awkward. The three of us stayed with my sister and her husband, sleeping on the floor of their apartment in Silverlake, near the park where John Lennon would go.

I was jerked awake in the night or early morning black by screams. I was dazed and filled with fear: where was I? what was going on? And then most importantly, were my child and wife safe? After an eternity of seconds I made sense: I was at my sister's; we were safe. Then I heard a car come to life in the distance and speed away in escape. None but me in the apartment had awakened. I then heard a neighbor's door open, and steps took off to do something.

The screaming woman had been raped. The neighbor had rushed to her far too late; even the cries had come after the rapist had fled. For moments in the dark I had tried to sort things, to establish what was what and then act. But it had all been too late; even the screams, the live screams, were a record of a violence past.

7 *days*

When I separated from my wife I returned once again to Los Angeles, this time from the San Francisco Bay area, from a house in San José and a job in Berkeley. I had Rockefeller money to spend a year at UCLA and write a book about time. I found myself in the city of my birth yet severed from family and home. And almost as disorienting, I found myself living in Westwood.

I think the fact of Westwood is not an insignificant factor in an affliction I acquired, which I came to call *dislocasia*. The disorientation I often felt upon waking, in the dizzy transition from sleep, came to be for me, rather than a transition, a lifestyle. For Westwood, that section of Los Angeles at the base of UCLA, Bel Air and Beverly Hills, between Hollywood and Santa Monica, strikes me as in essence off. And it isn't the matter of simulacra, the late twentieth-century dis-topos of philosophy that construes Los Angeles the great postmodern affair. I was born midcentury in the City of Angels, the simulacrum is home, and I can work up no particular awe for Hollywood, Disneyland or the Bonaventure, whether it be late capitalist, French, or paparazzi. It is the realness of Westwood that so managed to spin me hopelessly into confusion.

I was in B. Dalton Books on Westwood Blvd looking, I think, for some continuity from books, cleaved as I was from family and home in separation en route to divorce. After all, I seemed the same in bookstores, regardless whether they were in Bloomsbury or Westwood, and despite my fascination at their differences, the preponderance of Faber & Faber books, the methods of organization, the different magazines, I, nevertheless, seemed to myself about the same in each location, undertaking similar motions and expending similar time. I entered the bookstore from the LA winter of Westwood, a good summer for most places, simply to kill time. I lived on Levering, in Westwood, not so much walking as spitting distance from the cinemas and shops and my office on campus, a proximity I had never known in any city. At the travel section, I stared at guidebooks to Los Angeles and to San Francisco, reflecting that such a popular tourist and immigrant destination was what I called home. But then it struck me, which home?

I could not figure out which guide was appropriate because I did not know where I was. I had been struck by dislocasia. I spent a long, long time, perhaps all of twenty seconds, wondering where I stood, utterly fascinated at the blank I drew. Was it that synapses had blown, that I'd fallen off a weird topological fold, that I was dead, or that I had contracted physiological and psychological, spatial and temporal, dislocasia? I was to have numerous bouts with the disease over the next two years, most frequently when I'd wake up, like when I returned to Berkeley and moved into the house of men-without-their-children: the Puerto Rican with sons, preterit divorced; me, a Chicano with daughters, present progressive divorcing; and the Irishman with one of each, future subjunctive divorce. Occasionally the pre-dawn black transition from sleep to waking, and from pre motion to motion, would find me not recognizing anything. And at other times too, in daylight and in midsentence. Yet I had no panic and managed to find some small ironic pleasure at each occurrence: again? Ah, dislocasia.

Dislocasia's characteristic sense of nonlocatability and of being lost seems to me more profound than merely spatial. True, it manifested itself first and foremost as a break in contiguity, as a break in the sense of place, but it always made me feel as if I were displaced from a time line, as if the reason for the dislocation in space were caused in the first instance by a fall from the flow of one time to another.

One reason I could find some joy in spontaneous displacement is that it is such a break with the normal, for usually I have a very good sense of direction, of space and location. Another reason was its attendant sense of wonder.

I got lost on a walk in Mexico City once and quite enjoyed it. Quite simply, I made a wrong turn exiting a shop and zigzagged away in a wholly other direction than I realized or had intended. It was the summer in the middle of my twenties; two of my daughters had been born. I had gone to teach a course in Chicano literature but ended up studying Nahuátl with Juan Luna Cárdenas, an amazing man. I still recall him by his aphorism, "*cuando el indio encanece, el español ni aparece.*"

I left my wife and girls at our apartment for a walk, heading somewhere toward the aptly named Calle Niño Perdido. I didn't know Mexico City very well, so my excursions were still Hansel and Gretel bread crumb treks, paths I paid careful attention to so that I could retrace my steps back. I still conceived the city as linear paths with clearly ascribed destinations at each end, like the metros there or in Paris. I could not yet intuit DF as a field of inhabited zones crossed by a maze of streets.

I walked casually, absorbing impressions, confident in my orientation and sense of direction. I came to a bakery and wondered how Mexican Mexican bread could differ from Chicano Mexican bread. You see, *pan mexicano* is wonderful thing, and before I learned that it was a legacy of French imperialism (the cinco de mayo, Júarez, Maximilian, the French army), that it was an imitation of French pastry, I had long been fascinated by the distinct names, shapes, and textures of the individual pieces in the *panaderías* of East Los Angeles. So I walked into the bakery and absorbed the magic of bread.

When I exited I turned the wrong way, left or right, I do not recall, and found myself on streets I had never seen. That I was lost fascinated me: it was truly serendipitous and the surprise delighted me. And I truly was lost, for not only did I lose track of my trail of bread crumbs, but I was unable to conceive a larger picture of where I might be. I had lost my sense of line, and my sense of field was nonexistent.

When I first lived in London, I got around most often by tube rather than by walking or taking the bus. As a result I got to know the city very well, but for the longest time only according to the sense afforded by the tube lines.

When I switched to walking I was able to reconceive the city as a plane and as a field upon which I could envision other spatial relationships. It was as if my sense of the city expanded from the subterranean line to the surface plane, from lines with destination points to a grid of possibilities. For a bit in Mexico City, however, I seemed to exist only as a single point, amazed.

9 *flight*

While it is not true, I don't lie when I say that the reason I could not live in Ireland is because it is a land without hummingbirds. To think that I would live my days with the absolute impossibility of a chance sighting of one is, after all, a theoretical possibility. They are such magic and such joy I think in part because of how they fly: I think they must be to other birds what birds are to us. When I tried to describe them to Emer and explain why was her island so sad, I could only offer the fact that they could fly backward. It was as inadequate as it was inane, not my best expression as a poet.

I took off for Mexico to expunge a black hole I had placed in my soul while I was living in Westwood, in the days of dislocasia. I drove to Rosarito, Baja California, just beyond Tijuana. I like the border: it seems home to me, between the realities of Mexico and the US, a simulacrum perhaps, the way LA seems compared to Westwood, New York, London. Rosarito is a beach town, between Tijuana and Ensenada, less significantly a tourist destination than either.

I found a hotel on the broad beach at the end of a dirt road. I was the only guest. It was winter a few weeks after the big one in LA; the aftershocks were frequent, if irregular, shaking up things even this far south. The angry earth, the gray sky, and the solitary accommodation all increased the sadness of my spirit, or rather, if I were truly the center of the universe, as I sometimes suspect, earth, sky, and accommodation were sad and gray reflections of my spirit. I'd driven south because I felt like shit and wanted Mexico to fix me. It did.

I walked across the broad beach to the ocean's edge. Everything was gray with only the most muted trace of color. The water was gray, only slightly green; the sand was gray, distantly beige; the sky was gray and gray; I could find no trace of blue in it. There was a strong offshore blowing, and were it not invisible, I would have seen it blow gray against my black heart.

I stood at the edge of the water, turned my back on the sea, and looked back across the sand, face to the wind. The sand, I noticed, was not a single shade, but darker and lighter: blacker, heavy wet sand at my feet and whiter, airy light sand that never got wet in the distance. And in between the extremes there was a continuous spectrum of shade and moisture.

Birds must look at hummingbirds with wonder or with incomprehension at the least. I react to the ability to fly the way I imagine birds must to the ability to hover by the tiniest of their genus. No other bird can fly like the hummingbird; the others must wonder what it is like. In my dreams as a child and in my daydreams after, I wonder at the ability.

The strong offshore picked up the dry sand and blew it out to sea. At the water's edge, I could see the bright white sand blow toward me, over the darker and wetter sand and then by me, out to the sea beyond. In what must be a natural trompe l'œil, the whiter sand seemed to blow especially for me in a widening swath. The wind was stiff: I extended my arms as if wings. The lighter sand blowing over the darker, the noise of wave and wind, the wind itself, and me with wings: for a moment or two I knew what it was to fly. Much later, I related this to my mother; she said that these are moments given by god. An epiphany.

Once I was walking up Bancroft in Berkeley deep in thought when I was enveloped by intense fragrance. It was jasmine. When I turned to the bush, I caught sight of a tiny green hummingbird, darting, hovering, and doing the impossible. It seemed to me a gift, also an epiphany.

10 *fall*

I was sitting in the Nag's Head pub with Xóchitl, my middle daughter, then nineteen, the same daughter who five years earlier had beaten me up the Pyramid of the Sun at Tenochtitlan when the leading edge of my sole caught stone and humiliated me. I sat proud with my pint, she with her Orange Squash, proud that my daughter had found a great place to stay in London and that she was doing an admirable job at taking care of her life. As her father I marveled at the human irony that this young woman was the same younger teenager who left me in defeat on the side of a pyramid and the same little girl who rode her tricycle with the straightest of postures and yet too, the same child who at less than a year of age would respond to my question, "*¿Cuántos años tienes?*" with a loud "*¡Cero!*" She was yet Xóchitl even if different than she had been at any point along the narrative of her life. There in the pub with pride and with a pint or two, it seemed opportune to relinquish patriarchal authority for the narrative's meaning and to listen.

My daughter came back to our table in the corner, drinks in hand, eager to relate what the bartender had told her. Apparently the woman who cleared tables and occasionally brought drinks—it was a large pub—was the bartender's girlfriend and even more apparently, she had been speaking closely with some other guy and had even kissed him. Xóchitl, appearing to the bartender as a random opportunity for feminine exegesis, told him that such an action within his sight meant nothing serious. I, distanced by generation and gender, reserved judgment.

Anyway, as Chaos would have it, the objectionable guy came and sat at the table next to us, as remote a spot as the pub afforded. Out of nowhere the bartender's girlfriend appeared and glided over to his table. Her grace is significant in this retelling because on all other occasions that we'd seen her walk she demonstrated that gait Shakespeare noted of his race four centuries ago: "I grant I never saw a goddess go; / My mistress when she walks treads on the ground."

In the distance, the bartender strained to watch the couple every chance he could. Fortunately, their proximity was such that neither Xóchitl or I could avoid spying. They spoke about little, mostly the fencing of polite social intercourse, but their speech itself was charged with passion. Sadly, it seemed to me, hers more so than his. Yet I remained disinterested, my back to them, and read Xóchitl's silent expressions that marked significant locutions and gestures.

Enough was enough, however. The bartender came up to the couple in what Xóchitl explained was the most cool of ways: he just said hello. He waited for a response and then made light of the fact that some guy was off in the corner with his girl. Even I noted the labor in that pause, for not only was the woman the sort to be upset by surprise, she stumbled out a vague introduction that said nothing about her relationship with the bartender. The bartender took the hint and left, and so did the other guy, taking flight as soon as the bartender had withdrawn and polite society allows.

Hooked on this compelling story, Xóchitl and I settled in; we got more drinks and crisps, mint and lamb flavor by mistake, I think. The waitress cleaned up every ashtray in the pub, removed every glass and plate and utensil, and retreated to the back room for supplies or to adjust the thermonuclear control. She avoided the bartender like the plague. Since we were uninvolved except for the entertainment factor, it was for us sheer delight. Finally he caught her, but as Chaos would have it, it was across the room, well out of earshot. Fortunately, I sired a daughter for whom distance is no impediment and who gave me a blow-by-blow reading. The bartender gesticulated a bit, angry but calm; the woman looked down, maintaining the posture of guilt. After a while they went about their business, civilized. Show over, my daughter and I took off.

We had walked down Holloway Road to a cash box and after securing a fistful of pounds sterling were walking back in the direction of the pub. As we approached, the woman shot out, delight in face, running in abandon, almost as a child skips. Oblivious, she ran toward us and past, her face full of anticipation, joy even. Xóchitl and I looked at each other, "ah ha," she must be rushing off, covertly, to the other guy.

Then a sharp screech, a thud; we turned, and she lay in the middle of the road. Thinking I had to act, I sent Xóchitl to the pub to call an ambulance; I approached the fallen woman. She lay unconscious, peaceful as if asleep, but in a position like a chalked victim outline. A small silver-gray Japanese car poised just behind her, its windscreen shattered, sunken concave into the passenger compartment, completely fractured but holding still. The driver exited; he was dark, what goes for Paki in London, and extended his cellular phone to me. I waved him off and kneeled beside the still woman. There was no blood, she seemed asleep, dreaming; I put my hand to her shoulder; what else could I do? People gathered, some woman came up and adjusted the woman's skirt; I guess it had appeared somehow improper. Xóchitl came up and told me that at first she could only find the bartender in the pub and that she could not get herself to tell him his love lay mown down in the street. But she had managed something and help was on the way.

The police chased us off, so we went on with our lives. Late that night, we returned to the pub, and I inquired as to the woman's fate. To my amazement she was sitting at the bar and wearing the same clothes. She was ignorant of my concern, of my interest in a brief dramatic narrative in her life, and that at one point in my life it had seemed the most important thing to touch her, to kneel beside her and lay my hand on her shoulder.

11 *prince*

When Xóchitl was twelve, St. George's School in Kilburn was invited downtown to participate in an anti-drug campaign. The idea was to stage a "just say no" around Covent Garden before the media and aristocracy in a tacit expression of solidarity with Nancy Reagan. At the photo-op kicking off the crusade, my daughter and Tani, her African schoolmate, found themselves beside a prince. Foreigners both, they nonetheless stood there representing the abstinent youth of England, beside Edward. Tani extended her hand to shake his; Xóchitl did not, being too cool to do so. He dismissed the girl's gesture, declaring that if he allowed her to touch him, other would wish to do the same. I am proud to say that my daughter found that risible and found him to be such the dork.

So what translates in touch? I ask this not merely of the translation of different social forms of touch, in the manner of styles, but also of the physical link established by the touch. In one way, touching a prince, as well as touching a fallen English woman, is a matter of power. In England, unlike in India, being untouchable confers authority. To deny touch there is to exercise royal power. And yet on, or rather by, quite another hand, the stranger beside Ophelia in the pool of her own blood on Earl's Court Road conferred power. His touch said, "you do not need to get up, or panic, or struggle in the least: I'll be your strength."

And in regard to touch and knowledge: what better way to recognize the anachronistic decadence of a social system that confers power by gene than to listen to the laughter of a twelve-year old-Chicana?

At about the same time as the Edward-the-untouchable incident, I took a brief trip from London to Paris to Barcelona to Paris to London. It was all by surface and all in rapid succession. I visited a friend in Paris, lectured on Bakhtin in Barcelona, and then caught a lecture by Derrida on the rue d'Ulm on the way home. Travel by ferry or train is usually at such a pace that my sense of locasia has ample opportunity to adjust to each place. With air travel, however, the ready transition to place is not so much a function of the duration of flight, which is, after all, so brief, as it is that of the shock of airports, something akin to an alarm clock in a most perfect sleep: sharp, absolute, unforgiving.

Translation is most difficult, perhaps, with poetry and jokes. This is so, I believe, because both poem and joke are intricate plays of language, one aesthetic, the other humorous. Translation has been conceived tediously as an arrow shot from one language to the other, so that a Spanish arrow shot to an English target lands as "my aunt's feather is on the table," a bull's eye but alas, no joke. What is wrong with the metaphor is its disconnection, or rather, its connection by flight path alone, so that the context is severed from the content and the result hits or misses apart in the target language. Poets, joke tellers, and Chicanos keep track of language play by course so that metaphors other than spent arrows configure poem, joke, and border articulation.

My three-city, three-national-language tour brought to bear unexpected stress on my sense of linguistic play and translation. If I conceived translation both as an active interplay and as a conflictive spill between different languages, as in humor, for example, that could so make funny the claim of an embarrassed man in English that he is pregnant in Spanish, then I promulgated a model that could so easily spin out of control when subjected to rapid movement from England, France, and Spain, as it did. Because I am a Chicano poet who enjoys a good joke as well as a solid translation, I take delight in linguistic play and in linguistic interplay, in irony, ambiguity, parody, and dialogism, that is, in the push of the banal to poetry, to humor, or of humanity to the border. Such work is difficult enough in one language, very difficult in translation to a second, and exponentially more so, interactively among three.

My history is such that when I had gone to France or Spain it was most often from an English-speaking country. So the confluence of language was either English and French or English and Spanish. At least this was the case in Europe. In the Americas, the situation was more complex because I was born and raised in the borderlands where English and Spanish are mixed on both sides of an international frontier. In LA, for example, I took part in the play between, and in between, English and Spanish and Chicano hybrid speech. But away from this element, movement between languages in Europe meant that my focus was not so much on interplay as it was on practical translation, not on the play between but on the arrow from bow to target.

On the last leg of that three-city tour, I was preparing to return to England when I stopped at a post office in the cinquième. Having switched already from English to French, then French to Spanish, and then from Spanish to French all caught up with me there at the post office window. I lost myself in translation, awash in a stream of detached signifiers: *letter lettre letra carte-lettre carta post card carte postale postal tarjeta*. Unfortunately for the people in line behind me, I seized that opportunity to delight in the nonsensical dance of words and could communicate nothing intelligible to the counter person.

I dislike Eco's character Salvatore in *The Name of the Rose*, not because his hybrid language connotes heresy, but because the mixing of tongues denotes a mental deficiency for which he is burned at the stake. We live in times, after all, when Rita Patino Quintero can be confined to the Larned State Hospital for twelve years simply because hybrid speech is taken as sign of schizophrenia. At any rate, there at that moment in the French post office, I came to realize something about the play among words that I had undervalued at home in California, Alta as well as Baja. For not only the dynamics of play, but the spin on the inflection, the vantage point of the speaker, or perhaps more correctly, the site from which the speaker comes, participates in the meaning of the play. Place of origin could act to define the line of play in language as much as it does the trajectory of wind. Broken, confused, or lost, that trace of origin could lead to a heretic's death, a Chicana's incarceration, or a confused wait in line.

13 *the dead*

I spent my last teenage year among the dead, avoiding their bodies, afraid, and absolutely convinced that communication with them is impossible. The dead are not human, the corpse has the stillness of a photograph, the presence of stone. The dying human looks absolutely alive till death, then the body, absolutely dead.

To avoid Vietnam I went to college, and to pay for college I worked my sophomore year at the LA County Coroner's Office. It seemed ironic, during the times of a most ironic war, that my flight from killing abroad was to work as a custodian for the dead at home. I was a stock boy, which meant that I moved paper before it was written on and signed and thereby rendered official. The paper trail would take me by necessity, pushing my little cart, through the morgue, the place full of dead bodies, between my office and the storage room in the basement.

On the first day of work I confessed my fear of corpses to fellow student worker Chas T. He led me with our cart of forms through the morgue and told me to avert my eyes until he said we were clear. When he did we were beside a corpse, my first and a sight I recall to this day: the body of a tall woman, stiff as wood, and the color of Caucasian flesh transformed to a purple mahogany thing. I was as angry with him as I was shocked, all of which provided a sound beginning for friendship.

The Coroner's office seemed to me a hell for the detritus of humanity, the used up, discarded flesh that had been the indigent unable to die in a doctor's care, the assassinated presidential candidate, or the overdosed sex icon. We custodians too seemed similar, albeit living, detritus. The nonprofessional workers, those of us without degrees, were all minorities, mostly African-American. The doctors and technicians seemed to be either immigrants unable to practice in the US or Anglo-Americans, the sort of doctors from film noir, quirky and with secret pasts. The Coroner, who stayed in his office and whom I never saw except when he sent me to Philippe's for a lamb dip sandwich, was Japanese and regularly had it out with county higher-ups and the press.

Chas and I were left alone to regulate the flow of paper, left alone in accordance with the spirit of the place, which was a spirit of low-level compassion for fellow living humans. Unlike the dead, we shared a common vitality. We related to one another much the way Aussies and Kiwis do in

England, or Anglo-Canadians and Anglo-Americans do in a Slavic country. Chas and I would deliberately run low on some form or volunteer to secure a crate of gloves, so that we would take a county car and spend the day on the road. We would alternate such excursions at optimal frequency so as not to be denied the privilege. Our access to the car, freedom from the workplace, and attempts at cavalier attitudes made us the self-proclaimed gifts to the young female clerical staff. Young, because the older Black women dismissed us as boys.

We each had our favorite excursions as well as those we undertook simply because we were paid to do so. I had two favorites: one with Jill, to El Tepeyac, and the other with Bonnie to the USC medical center at LA County General. Manuel's El Tepeyac is a prime Mexican restaurant in East Los, situated ironically beside the Evergreen Cemetery and close enough to downtown to fill with suits at lunch. To this day I take delight in upsetting the bourgeoisie, but Jill was restless and easily bothered by the righteous, those aghast that her black body was not seated across another equally so. Bonnie, the only young and Anglo woman among the secretaries, was from Greeley, Colorado, on an urban hiatus of sorts. She'd wait in the car while I'd rushed into the hospital for a box of rubber gloves, then we'd park somewhere high in Lincoln Heights, overlooking a freeway, and talk and laugh. On other occasions, I would acquiesce to drive to the printer's, a most boring trip, a short drive that required a long wait, far too long to bring anyone along and too boring to laugh.

Throughout that time among dead, I believed that talk with the body was not possible even though touch was. The Hall of Justice is a shady gray cube of a building, a solid testimony to order overlooking the Santa Ana Freeway. It is the house of justice for social detritus: there are cells for felons, courts for their judgment and sentencing, sheriff's deputies to marshal restraint, and on the ground, if you entered from Spring Street, it was the work place for the custodians of the dead. From Broadway, the Coroner's was one-level subterranean.

I avoided the portentous entrance down from Broadway, preferring instead the portal on Spring, flush with the surface as it was and suggesting life and a season of creation. By my last days there, the end of the summer I'd leave LA, my struggles to remain on the level with life in the house of the dead had been marked, over and again, by signs of the dead.

Like for example the sign of the X, not of the cross, but of the letter, as in X marks the spot. They were three, girls my age, hanging around at the Spring Street entrance. Chas took no interest in white hippie chicks, but Lewis, the Jewish artist from Berkeley, did, so he and I would take our breaks, and he his lunch times as well, with them. The three girls milled, killing time, waiting outside in the daylight for the verdict of the big trial going on within. We liked them, but I lost interest when they shaved their heads and carved X's in their foreheads. Lewis on the other hand had fallen in love and had been invited to the Spahn Ranch: what did I think, should he go? To this day, I would find romance difficult with the devotee of a murderer or at the site of ritual killing.

But how could Lewis not be confused there in the light of day? He had, after all, the most claustrophobic of jobs at the Coroner's, toiling away all summer in the back of a vault beneath the morgue. His place was marked off from the rest of the office as the final repository for the last detritus of the long dead. For after the body had undergone autopsy and had been sent off for funeral, and even after the still remains that had housed the human spirit had long since decayed, Lewis managed the care of its ultimate piece. His job consisted of opening jars that had exceeded their five-year shelf life, emptying their contents into special bags and throwing the jars into other special bags. The contents of the jars were small bits of the dead: an embryo, a gall stone, and various other well catalogued but unrecognizable fragments that had once been vital. The Coroner's care of the dead continued well beyond the autopsy; words were stored on paper and body bits in jars. Above at ground level, I ensured the supply of blank forms; below in the basement, Lewis disposed of the last physical trace.

To visit Lewis at work I would pass through the morgue and do my best to avoid perceiving by any of my five senses an infant on the floor scale, a mahogany body, or a mass of decomposition that had been human a couple of weeks before being locked up in the trunk of a car. Down in the underground without windows and amid tunnels lay Lewis's dark cell. It hid beside the overflow room, which was actually a room-sized refrigerator for those times of natural or unnatural mass death, and the Sheriff's vault for confiscated drugs. You could smell marijuana, thick, emanating from behind the heavy door but no custodian of the dead had access to that space. What was accessible, however, was the storage room for the unclaimed effects of the dead: a room of brown envelopes, each containing what had been in the possession of humans at the moment of death. And of course, many of them did die holding onto drugs. Lewis would tear into envelope after envelope and take marijuana joints, pills, lots of pills, and whatever else smacked of contraband. We would retire to the far reaches of his cell to talk. He'd ingest whatever he found, and we'd watch the occasional deputy cross by the door.

By the end of that summer, I had borne witness to many signs of the dead, which had, for no clear reason, entwined words with bits of flesh. When Oscar Zeta Acosta came through, one of the Black secretaries pointed out "the Chicano lawyer" to me, so that I could see one of my own, the only one, who entered the place with any authority, Zeta had come to confront the authorities in a routine matter, the death of a Chicano in police custody. In *Revolt of the Cockroach People*, Zeta describes that visit to the Coroner's and how he gathered evidence by directing the severing of bits of flesh from the body of Robert Fernández. Zeta ends the novel recalling the police killings of Fernández and of Rubén Salazar.

My job ended when I came into work where Salazar's body had been brought in, after having been there when he was killed. I had been there when an LA County Sheriff deputy killed Rubén Salazar, there in a general, yet most profound sense, for I did not find out till later how the tear gas projectile that had been designed to pierce walls had ripped through his life in the Silver Dollar Cafe on Whittier Boulevard. I was there somewhere down the street, being chased by police who were shooting tear gas canisters from the ground and dropping them from helicopters. Salazar and I were both there as journalists: he was the most eminent voice for Chicanos, a journalist for the *LA Times* and KMEX television; I was freelancing for the *LA Free Press*. But I survived, and hedid not. Afterward I ensured that there was paper for my boss to record the cause of death, a "projectile wound of the left temple area causing massive injury to the brain."

15 *gun*

So when the police had my daughter in an assassination position, kneeling, gun to her head, I took care to choose and phrase my words precisely. I pulled into the driveway when Junior, son of the deaf couple next door, ran up to me saying the police had Marisol at the end of the block. I wonder about Junior's self-articulation, being as he was mixed, half Chicano, but raised completely without the sounds of parental words in any language.

There were two policemen, a man and a woman, Anglos both; the man had the pistol at my daughter's head. My wife came up to me as I reached the scene. Both policemen watched us speak, watched the brief exchange by what was taken for an irrational Mexican mama and whatever I was to prove to be.

I never did write the article about the police riot and the destruction on Whittier Boulevard that culminated in the deaths of Gilberto Díaz, Lyn Ward, and Rubén Salazar. The *LA Free Press*, radical journal that it was, had had plenty of eyewitness and analysis, so in the face of such quantity there was no need for my piece. A week before it did run a piece of mine that described an upcoming demonstration, what was to become the largest Chicano protest against the war. But the description of the event itself, of the chaos and the killing, I did not write because of a loss of faith. You see, the news reports, especially those on television, lied, not merely slanted in bias, but outright lied about wild Chicano radicals and innocent peace officers. I lost faith in truth, in the hard link between world and event.

So I extended what police want: absolute acquiescence: it was a small price for my daughter's brain left intact. I addressed the pig in my very best rational liberal humanist, Protestant work ethic individualist, law-abiding and God-fearing all-American speech. I put to the test the PhD and years of watching television. I did my best to speak my daughter out of insignificance and to move her image in his mind to an equivalency with that of a suburban Anglo girl of the bourgeoisie, the national icon he would be loathe to kill.

In the end I spoke well but did nothing. I think that had I not lost faith as a young man in East Los Angeles, I might have lost a daughter that day in San José.

16 *faith*

I spent the first years of my life in East Los Angeles and my school years down the boulevard, farther east in Whittier. In between those two homes, I spent the fourth year of my life in Montebello, just off Beverly Boulevard. From that time and space, an interstice in my personal narrative, I recall two blood incidents, very small incidents, but ones that did foster a particular faith that I was to lose much later.

The first incident is as brief as it is vague: my sister threw a toy rifle at me, hitting me on the ear; I remember almost nothing else but bleeding and a texture of wound. The second is a more developed story, reflecting, I think, its greater significance in the narrative of my life. María Luísa, or Tata, as she was called, used to bite me. She did this often and with neither mercy nor provocation. She'd bite into my arm, for example, and no matter what I'd do, she would not let go until she so pleased. In truth, my protestations were weak; they were verbal except for the physical attempts to break free. I took very seriously my mother's prohibition against hitting girls. As a result, I was repeatedly punctured and indented and made to cry. Finally, in a scene I recall reminiscent of a Bruce Lee film, my mother relented and authorized, no, rather demanded the use of violence. The next time Tata bit me, I pushed her off and chased her. I picked up a shard of glass and cut her back as she ran away screaming.

There is a lesson in violence, and it is called upon to justify its use: violence can put an end to some action. As much as I would like to decry this with a rebuttal like violence only exacerbates, or something of the sort, I don't because, in truth, Tata never bit me again, Rubén Salazar never wrote again and, in illustration of its absence, a daughter of mine persists to this day because violence was not employed.

17 *fear*

Fear, unlike violence, is a slow burn. While a gunshot, cut, or rape happens with brilliant intensity, it is bounded by its absence. Fear, on the other hand, is a long story with a long blur of suffering and the longing for release. For this reason it seems often spatial, an emotion attached to a location: a bedroom, the ghetto, hell. And it is also for this reason rendered temporal: a fear of old age, night, the moment before going on stage. Its extension across space and time, as well as the familiar delineation of fears in story lines, gives the emotion a particular palpability. We assign meaning to its presence, dimension, and direction when we attach fear to place, time, to thing. Our sense of fear is its link, the connection we sense between the irrational and its object.

Twice in poems I took up the matter of fear. That both were long poems, prosey, and of similar tone seems to me to indicate that I find such form appropriate for such content. I wrote "*À mon seul désir*" in two voices, one lyric, the other prosaic, one masculine, the other feminine, yet all in Spanish except for its French title. The title serves for me as the link, necessary for an evocation of the emotion, with a particular place, time, and object. It is a poem as much about fear as it is about a life, as much about an irrational undercurrent as it is about a real walk.

It was winter in Paris, early February; the streets were wet, the air, cool, heavy. Two of us had time to kill, so Dominique decided to show me a bit of her city. The night before, there had been a disagreement among friends: three women and an Australian emigrant argued the oldest church in Paris. I watched them go at it, silently, lacking as I was in local knowledge, but hoping that St-Julien-le-Pauvre beat out St. Germain-de-Prés because I so liked the poor name. And as it turned out, my walk with Dominique did take me to very old religious sites, yet the matter in contention remained unresolved.

We walked by the Tour St-Jacques, the odd ruins of a church, a solitary corner, standing as if it had been meant to be a tower. We wandered into the end of an evening mass. And we went to the Musée de Cluny, the site of old Roman baths and a museum of medieval art. It is there that a most famous set of Lady and Unicorn tapestries hangs. The tapestries are of a piece, six hangings, one to each of the senses and a sixth, "*À mon seul désir . . .*" Their story, I imagine, is a rejection of the worldly in favor of the divine, played out in the rejection of the perceptible, one sense at a time. The ultimate object of desire is unclear, however, because the title piece, "to my one desire . . .," is not completely legible: a final letter remains indecipherable as if a vague initial of the absent object of desire.

By the time we stood before the tapestry, Dominique and I had spent enough time walking together, sharing sights, and absorbing the signs of French Catholicism that it was easy to turn the focus to ourselves. I was very much taken by the tapestry's flat perspective that surrounded the yellow-haired Lady with fantastic animals on a single plane. I pointed out a strange representation of a bird, and Dominique confided her fear of birds, a fear such that she would not eat them. It was not a profound fear; it was a casual one, casual yet real. Its object struck me as comical, impossible as such, of course, because it was not a fear specifically my own.

Dominique resembles the Lady in the "*À mon seul désir . . .*" tapestry, blonde, pale, and thin, similar but without the unicorn and in twentieth-century dress with green eyelashes. And why not? The story of a denial of the senses and an embracing of an elusive desire is woven into the fabric of her race, as much as it is woven into her individual story: in presence and dimension and object of fear. And I am touched by that emotion when I recall the ambient elements of color, moisture, fabric, and a present but unintelligible object of emotion.

18 *being*

The subject of expression, both in subject as agent and as in subject matter, works and works out differently in lines of lyric and in lines of story. Given a like object in writing of poetry and prose, the realization of desire, for example, the fact of method of each yields disparate results. Take for example the issue of ontology.

A common story of the becoming of a writer of narrative is one of living a life in narration. Accomplished fiction writers from George Orwell to Sandra Cisneros have explained a curious phenomenon in their youth. It seems their future call was evidenced in a self-conscious narration of their banal acts. That is, as they undertook some action, walking up stairs, for example, they narrated their actions to themselves silently as if reading description in a novel. An odd and, in truth, somewhat tedious undertaking to my mind, which I'm sure so occurs to me because god did not make me to write fiction.

That fiction writers would look back upon life as if it were a narrative sequence of events that lead casually to their present makes sense because they are fiction writers. Notwithstanding my employment of tautology, it is in character for fiction writers to both conceive and depict the human being as a line of unfolding causes and effects. That their formation should be described in a personal narration is appropriate and demonstrates a fundamental faith in an essential fabric of writing and being. I think that the world must make sense for them as an ontology of sequence, that one becomes in order.

So if in life the fiction writer reaches for a door and narrates the sequence of events as they occur, what does the poet do? To answer that the poet reaches for the door and thinks *more* or *Othello* may point to something. But to merely insert a poetic break in a sequence of narrative logic is an attempt to figure the poetic in the line of the prosaic. Something of the opposite happens when one seeks to define metonymy with synonym, that is, seeks metaphors for metonymy. But then if we subtract narration, what are we left in the conception and description by the poet? Perhaps we are left with an emphasis on image rather than a story. If the object of desire is left illegible in "*À mon seul désir* . . . ," what is the domain of that object? Are those French words poetry? fiction?

During my first winter after leaving Los Angeles, I found myself in Santa Cruz attending a reading by Galway Kinnell. He read his bear poems, masculine verse about hunting and killing and surviving in nature. After reading one poem, he explained in casual commentary how he had invented the method of killing the bear, that of freezing a bone curved in meat so that it would thaw, uncurl, and rip the insides of the bear that ate it. Clever, I thought, but somewhere there seemed to be a lie. In the middle of his reading it began to snow: I could see white flakes against the dark redwoods outside. I had just left LA and had never seen snow fall from the sky. I pondered: should I finish the reading or see the snow. I went outside and caught flakes in my hands my hair and my life for the first time.

Let me digress here. I have remained interested in a line of thought, whether it manifest as a progression toward the absent object of desire, as a connection to the fragmentary and dead, or as a structure for an emotive logic. Meaning, it seems, given dimension, direction, and impetus, accrues. Yet besides considering linear movements from point A to point B and on to C, one can well ask, literally, how fast?

In auto racing there is a virtual line on the race track, an optimum path to realize maximum speed. But that is not quite correct, for the line is taken to yield the least elapsed time. Yet inasmuch as the consideration of the distance over time can be expressed as the ratio *speed*, less time means greater speed. But the fact remains that the race is won by the one who crossed the finish line first, in the least time, regardless of any speed along the way. A line is therefore driven that permits the circumvention of the track with the expenditure of the fewest fractions of seconds.

Tracks for road racing combine straights and turns and changes in elevation and slant. The course of a lap can include straights of varying lengths; turns, left and right; curves of various arcs, with decreasing or increasing radii; elevation changes in the length of the course and slope changes across its width: a menagerie of the chicane, esses, hairpin, carousel, and off-camber. But for all its variation, the road course is a single surface, turning, rising, falling, but never leaving the track plane. The race car's line is flat on the pavement; it is not like the line of the airplane or the swimmer underwater. And across that flat track plane, the racer works out the shortest time line.

That line does mark a time sense for the circuit: it defines the track from edge to edge with the sole purpose to cut time. Toward that end, the driver can do little to control distance, a lap after all being a lap, and so is left with the only other variable in the equation: speed. And so to diminish time and the duration of the race, the driver rationally follows a line of maximum speed. In general, the rule of the line is that most time is cut on the straights, and so it is essential to take them at maximum speed. Corners become slingshots from which cars are thrown into straights, and so the racing line becomes the path of the fastest exiting speed from the corners leading to straights.

Because of this, driving a race is something quite different from driving the streets. On rigorous road courses at maximum speed there is little of the sense of casual motoring. First, there is the matter of commitment to the line. At maximum speed the car is at the very edge of control; the balance of a car in a high speed corner can easily be lost by simply changing lines or applying the brakes. Each lap is a set sequence of optimum shifting, braking and cornering points with little rational opportunity for variety. Second, there is the matter of constraint. The driver, especially in formula cars, is tightly wedged into the race car. The driver must shoe horn deep in the cockpit and cannot see his knees, let alone his feet. He can only see behind and to the side by the use of the two tiny side mirrors. He is held pressed into the seat by a six-pointed star of belts, and his entire body, except for the eyes, is covered in flame-retardant material. Blood type must be displayed on the suit.

I didn't race much because of the cost and eventually sold the car for the down payment on a house. Yet one residual benefit to this day from racing is the particular bond I formed with my youngest daughter. When I worked on the car, endless hours taking it apart completely, Mireya would often accompany me. She was in diapers and would stand on the seat, grip the small steering wheel, and listen to me describe camber, sway, or the appropriate Hewland ratios. I thought she was fascinated by the stuff and that I was imparting carbon monoxide receptivity and a love for the sport. It wasn't until I next got to Willow Springs that I found out her interest was not in racing and not even in the car, but rather in the steering wheel itself. Its leather cover had proved irresistible for my teething offspring, and she had gnawed her way through.

Turn nine at Riverside was a long, sweeping right hander at the end of a long straight just before the esses. This meant it was a fast turn: you entered it at top speed, very little scrubbed off, and you shot out barely able to ride out the quick left, right, left. The turn itself was broad and banked, giving the illusion that you could motor casually across its width. But at the end of the straight, you entered it as fast as your car could go; that straight, after all, was where you most ate the clock. The corner was rimmed by a low concrete wall, which seemed to race with you through the turn as you held tight to the line. It was the wall's absolutely unforgiving concrete that awaited those who strayed off line and that had grown men scream in their helmets there lap after lap.

I pushed the blue formula car into the straight after badly negotiating an off-camber left-hander: I never seemed to get set up right for the long straight. But I'd get on the straight and go, up the gears, right foot to the floor. I'd pass and be passed on that straight and then fall into turn nine. I'd push the car till the rear wheels were about to break loose and hold on. In my peripheral vision, I'd watch the wall running beside me, marking the absolute edge of my track. In the low, single-seat car, I saw, or rather reclined, so my eye level was less than three feet above the pavement. The wall was a bit taller. As I approached the end of the turn, I knew my line would take me from the inside right to the outside left edge when I exited, that is, toward the wall. At the exit, everything would speed up. The fast turn seemed calm till its end, then, in a rush across the track to the exit of the turn, it looked as if the wall came rushing up to me. Every time I exited that turn, lap after lap, I'd watch that wall, and every time, I came close, inches at most, from hitting the edge of the wall, and yet every time, I shot out beyond, off into the esses.

While the car may be an instrument for linear motion on the road course of a single plane, meaning can be ascribed by a recourse to other levels, higher and lower. This after all is a trick of humanity: any act undertaken or object envisioned can be considered from remove. The real and down-to-earth movement from green flag to checkered, or from one neighborhood to another in the city, can come to mean life. For if memory divided by place is the ratio of experience, it is precisely by undertaking the drive that we arrive at meaning. And the more intense the experience, the more meaningful our life story.

The other plane from which we reflect upon our linear motion can be, at times, the very fabric of life itself. Consider two drives, one in the high desert north of LA, the other in the city.

I particularly like the track at Willow Springs because of its terrain. It is at the base of a hill in a wide expanse of desert. The track wanders up and down and around without the need for crash walls: if you spun out on the hill side, gravity would prevent you from going so far; if you did on the plain side, the very worst would be a long walk back through tumbleweed. The desert offered a measure of security, for upon losing control and falling away from the racing line, drivers would confront nothing but absent expanse.

One weekend, for diversion, they ran the races in the opposite direction. This effectively created a new track: the traditional line was useless, and I had to spend the practice sessions trying to plot a new one. The race came all too soon, and I found myself with just the most sketchy idea of a line. I did not have the comfort of clarity, the sure knowledge of well-defined breaking points and corner apexes. Going the other way, the history of the course was annulled; even the streaks of black rubber across the corners meant nothing.

At one point, I decided on a strategy based on a weak logic. I put faith in an algebraic or empirical sense of equivalency: Formula Ford equaled Formula Ford, therefore I could take the same line at the same speed and experience the same results as any other. I tucked the blue Winklemann FF in line behind a black Merlin FF at the end of the straight and followed it into the broad left-hander that had been, in the track's former incarnation, the sweeping right-hander that led to the long straight. The black car delayed braking longer than I would have and took a turning point farther into the turn as well. I followed and lost it.

As I turned into the turn, the rear wheels broke loose, sending the tail of the car out sideways as if in race with the front. I corrected, but it was too late.

About crashing in formula cars, there are several points. First, it is rare to go airborne. Unless you ride over the wheels of another car, the chances are you will spin round and round until some law of physics makes you stop. Second, speed is not the issue. The cars do not have speedometers, and performance is measured by a legion of timekeepers to the ten thousandth of a second. And besides, during the spin the control the driver exercises over direction and rate is completely gone. And third, race cars are hard to start, so once you are spinning out of control the best you can do is to hold on, put in the clutch, and give it some gas so as not to kill, at least, the motor.

So I did just that, gripped the then useless-for-steering wheel, and tried to keep the motor alive. I also closed my eyes. I could see no use for vision at the time. Eventually after a most spectacular spin, which began, incidentally, at well over a hundred miles per hour, I came to a stop in a great cloud of dust. There was dirt in my eyes and inside the balaclava, in my mouth and thick in the air so that I had no idea where I was. Was I outside the track, halfway to Las Vegas; inside the track; or was I, horror, still on the track? And the motor was dead. Would a car or two or more come shooting in the cloud and smash into me? Crashing was not a main fear of mine, but fire, being trapped in a burning car, was. I thanked god that the gas tank between the motor and me, maybe three inches behind me, held only five gallons. I wore a suit that would retard burning for fifteen seconds, so what was five gallons?

Then I got hit on the helmet two times: it was a corner worker, fire extinguisher in hand. I could see him standing beside me; the dust cleared. I was in the dirt, inside, and more importantly, off, the track. He motioned, was I OK? I hit the starter button and surprise, the motor came to life. I put it in first, and spun great plumes of dirt and got back into the fray.

It was an epiphany of sorts, for I knew then that I was immortal. Or perhaps not quite, but I knew that death would not take me unless I relented at least partially.

A few years earlier in Los Angeles I drove a VW bug on a short drive from City Terrace to Lincoln Heights, neighborhoods that straddle the San Bernardino Freeway. I was in the offices of La Raza Unida, the political party and radical journal, when a call came in from the offices of Los Tres del Barrio: bring cameras; the police were about to begin shooting. There were only three of us in the office; it was late. And because we were young, none of us veteranos of the movement, we said we'd go and did.

The drive is short, literally just across the freeway, but at that time the distance from Raza Unida to Los Tres was measured in ideological miles. The three of us jumped into my sister's beige VW with the intention to bear witness. We were political activists and believed literally in a *raza unida*. Whoever called us probably had been the same: naive, enthusiastic, and not yet embittered by real-world politics. Actually, it hadn't been that long since both organizations struggled together, but at that later moment our drive was more like one between antagonistic Chicano neighborhoods, which it was, from Varrio Geraghty Lomas to Hazard. Yet while the three of us clearly identified as Raza Unida and did our political work in Lomas, we saw no reason not to go.

We got there in a matter of minutes, the last glow of daylight quickly vanishing. None of us had ever been to the offices of Los Tres; we felt like war correspondents going to bear witness for the raza. We found the office at the base of a slope, across the street from an open space of grass and palm trees. A crowd had gathered out front, perhaps sixty or so of all ages, clearly not just the college radicals, but the neighborhood folk as well. I drove the VW with great caution, for as we neared we saw the police vehicles and, one by one, marksmen in riot gear became visible behind the trees. Police raids of Chicano offices, those of La Raza Unida or the Brown Berets, for example, were common fact. And Los Tres seemed to warrant a special attention because it existed to defend three Chicanos, Alberto Ortiz, Juan Fernández and Rudy Sánchez, imprisoned for shooting and paralyzing an undercover narcotics officer, Bobby Canales.

The drive itself seemed unreal, like a drive in fog I once took in Santa Cruz, which inspired a poem that took twenty years to complete. It seemed to pass silently, very, very slowly, as if we were still and it was the world that gyrated almost imperceptibly outside. We passed the marksmen and let them see our faces, the license plate, and did what you are supposed to do before killers: look them in the eyes and promise to remember. For whatever reason the operation was called off, and the police retreated for another day. We had not stopped nor had needed to; we bore witness to life from the confines of a car driving in circles.

There was a time, over the matter of a few days, that I traveled to Northern Italy and to Northern Ireland in the hospitality of women amid terrorists. I was living in Sligo at the time, so the journey to Italy was by air through London after a drive to Dublin. The journey from Sligo to Northern Ireland was simpler, an easy drive three hours east. I visited the graves of the tragically dead, Juliet Capulet in Italy and Bobby Sands in Northern Ireland, and in Belfast I was attacked by a tree.

I went to Italy to read poetry in Milan and in Treviso, which is just inland from Venice. It was at the time of the Biennale, the big European arts festival that is held in Venice, as the name implies, biannually. The reading in Milan was a tiny affair at a bookstore not far from the galleria. The reading in Treviso was well attended, the last in the series, *rosso de sera*.

I read in English and in Spanish with an Italian translator at my side. Except for the requisite lag, being translated at the moment proved a delightful yet curious phenomenon. I'd read then pause. The audience would look to Elena for the Italian version of the English but would tend to stay focused on me through the Spanish. After the readings in both cities there was a period for questions, a feature not often the case in the readings I've done before English-speaking audiences in the US or Ireland. The period of questions and answers seemed to make for an air of greater intimacy because of the presence of the translator: she was our living icon, testifying to our characteristically human struggle to understand and be understood.

All of which was particularly interesting in Italy. My poems are interlingual poems, mostly English or Spanish or English and Spanish, but some decidedly more complex. In short, they are border poems, playing in the linguistic terrain characteristic of the zones of international frontiers. So translation of a sort is a dynamic central to my verse. And inasmuch as my poems delight in a give and take across languages, both in form and in content they seemed to hold themselves up to the Italians as self-articulating artifacts, self-consciously inviting participation. Be that as it may, it was more the Italian audience than the poems themselves that shaped the course of the reading: they had read selections from *Cantos* in translation and were poised to interrogate and criticize. My work had appeared in Italian in a literary journal devoted to the politics of poetry. *Baldus* takes its name from an early modern macaronic poet who combined Latin and the vernacular, and so in a sense, my work found a welcome home there. There was a sense of intimacy, one that centered around the desire to come to grips with the impossible task we undertake when we try to understand one another. When I left the Treviso reading and had late dinner with the host poet and his mother, I was told that an epigraph from a poem of mine had been used to mark the entrance to a section of paintings at the Biennale. That, the interest in my work, and an argument over what Lombards purport to be fresh mozzarella in the north, left me moved and thoroughly taken with the place.

On our drive back to Milan, Elena pulled the red Volkswagen off the highway in Verona to show me the *tomba Giulietta*. I am fascinated by the great manifestations of human spirits in places such as cathedrals and the tombs of fictional characters. Both cathedral and tomb, after all, attest to our humanity and affirm in celebration of the species. In the way that the Sistine chapel can impress the atheist with the sense and passion of faith, and by the way, I find the question of whether or not the nonbeliever comes to believe not interesting, in that way, the real place and the physical effects of fictional characters affect me profoundly. And what it is that so strikes me is the fact of desire.

The tomb of Romeo's beloved lies in the center of a dark room in a renaissance building. The tomb looks like a stone bathtub in the middle of the floor. That I was not the first to make pilgrimage is evident by the bits of paper. In the alcove and the slits for light there are testaments to romance: tiny notes on metro tickets, pages from address books, and torn envelopes, truly not professions of faith, but statements of desire. Most were written in Italian, mostly by women, yet all written in the hand of one in love, one having lost love or not having received love. They declared hearts' desires; they made affirmations before the tomb of the tragically dead lover. On occasion they asked Juliet to intercede. I don't think they are motivated the same way that motivates the pilgrim at Tepeyac, Lourdes, or Mecca, for there really isn't faith at their core. What there is, is desire. And who can say which is stronger, faith or desire? In the dark of a small room in Verona, there is ample testimony to the human power of desire.

In Belfast I took my daughters to Milltown Cemetery to visit the grave of Bobby Sands. There is a poem by Sharon Doubiago that juxtaposes his tragic story, a long withering away, of death by starvation, with the cruel irony of decadent life continuing at the same moment. "Hunger" traces the story of the 217-day series of hunger strikes at Maze prison from March 1 to October 3, 1981, which resulted in 10 deaths: Bobby Sands, dead after 66 days of hunger; Francis Hughes, 59 days; Raymond McCreesh, 61 days; Patsy O'Hara, 61 days; Joe McDonnell, 61 days; Martin Hurson, 45 days; Kevin Lynch, 71 days; Kiernan Doherty, 73 days; Tom McElwee, 62 days; and Mickie Devine, 69 days. "Hunger" details the starvation of 10 bodies, 10 Irishmen whose desire to live free was realized by the final power left the weak, that to say no even to their own flesh. Against this, the poem juxtaposes the English desire for power and the power of desire in the fairy tale wedding and honeymoon of Princess Diana, which took place in the middle of the death strike.

Bobby Sands died on cinco de mayo 1981 and is buried in the IRA section of Milltown, in a plot for three. A headstone marks the site: VOLUNTEERS / TERENCE O'NEILL / BOBBY SANDS / JOE MCDONNELL. The plot is plainly formal, bordered by a teal railing, adorned by small flowers and ribbons in the tricolor of the republic. That it is so dressed up is somehow fitting, for Bobby's death was the culmination of protests that began with an incident about dress. In 1976, Ciaran Nugent demanded recognition as a political prisoner and refused to wear a prisoner's uniform. From this sprang the blanket protest at Maze prison: three and a half years wearing only blankets and living in awful conditions. The protesters were confined to bare cells, and in response to having their food thrown in by the guards, they smeared their excrement on the walls. Three and a half years wearing blankets and living in shit. This action cumulated in a hunger strike, from October 27 to December 18, 1980. Only after this and after facing the options available to those with power only over their own bodies, they resolved to strike for recognition or until death. Sands and the other nine starved, while the English and American media delighted in the story of a princess and a prince and the ritual reproduction of a system of gene supremacy that the enlightened parts of the world had cast off long ago.

My friend Camille took us to Milltown and pointed out the names and dates on stone in a long history of resistance. She pointed where Michael Stone came up from the highway with automatic weapon and grenades and attacked a group of mourners, wounding fifty and killing three. She told us of many other deaths, of deaths by mistakes of all sorts. She described the facts of apartheid and took us through housing projects very much like Pico Gardens or Maravilla in East LA: poverty, segregation, police surveillance, and cultural nationalist murals. Camille, Sharon Doubiago, and I all had been raised in Los Angeles but only Camille had emigrated and made Belfast her home. She and I had gotten to know each other in Berkeley and as she says, emphasizing the irony, despite the bombings and the harassment she gets from British soldiers, she is safer in Belfast than she was in Oakland. Statistically she is correct. What does this say about my life, about my daughters' lives? I had heard Bernadette Devlin once talk about this irony of safety amid terror, life amid death.

At one point my daughters and I found ourselves waiting for Camille to come out of class. We sat on a low brick wall at the entrance to Queen's University, on the aptly named University Road. The day was pleasant if a bit too gray and cool for summer. While waiting, I thought about violence and colonialism and the fortress called a police station that overlooks Belfast's Catholic barrio. I wondered about the university: it must, after all, be the Queen's, not merely in name, but owned personally by Elizabeth, the way Hyde Park and the Falkland Islands are. I was feeling particularly Catholic there at the portal to the Protestant university when all of a sudden out of nowhere I was struck in the face and in the groin. I recoiled in pain but could make absolutely no sense. Then I figured it out: there at my feet lay a thick hunk of royal branch, a small log, I like to think. Apparently, Elizabeth's tree had attacked me, crashing first into my mouth and then my genitals. What did it mean? Was this a natural expression in a country without freedom of speech? Was I being censored so as to neither reproduce textually or sexually?

My two friends in Northern Ireland and Northern Italy have lived close to terrorists. Camille's husband served prison time for his activities but has given up violence and works instead on cultural change. He teaches Irish language and culture in a center that looks very much like similar Chicano organizations. Elena's boyfriend's brother has served a longer sentence. He remains proud that he neither informed nor recanted, both of which are heavily desired by the Italian police. On the flight from the land of one friend to that of the other, I sat next to a Spanish woman, María, who worked for a Formula One organization in London. My surname, she noted, is Basque, which in Spain signifies ethnic minority and ETA, the nationalist, separatist organization, and terrorism. However we did not speak of terror but rather of desire and poetry.

22 *color*

Desire in painting must be nothing like desire in poetry. Color too, must be different. I find it hard to imagine desire painted, a depiction of its object perhaps, presented in the color of blood. Desire seems verbal, textual, to me: a novel of lust, a lyric of lack. This might well be because I work in words and envision the world in their terms. And so color in my poems must miss the color spread on canvas the way word and phrase are never pigment but the word and phrase for pigment.

I went to a show of work by Frida Kahlo at the Mexican Museum in San Francisco. Along with retablos and portraits, undoubtedly as the curator's supplement, were words: excerpts from Frida's diary printed huge on the walls beside the paintings. My job as a poet prescribes that I pay attention to words, and I was drawn to those of this painter, but beyond this, I was particularly taken because I so often wonder what of an artist transcends media.

My experience of bearing witness to artists' expression in alternate media has been associated with death. I arrived in Paris days after Julio Cortázar died and thereby forever missed the opportunity to see him play jazz. And when I was twenty, my friend Tad and I made a pilgrimage from Santa Cruz to Kenneth Patchen's house in Palo Alto. He was too near death to receive visitors, but his wife gave us a small stack of postcard-sized reproductions of his poem paintings, or painted poems, whichever they were. And of course by the time I stood in San Francisco before the excerpts from Frida Kahlo's diary, she had long since died.

I grew excited when I realized what Frida's text was. At last I could get insight into the transition across media from color to word and into the meaning of color for the painter. For there before me, huge on the wall, were Frida's definitions of colors. For me, colors were words, verbal images, tropes perhaps, hypertext links to meanings of colors. When I meant green, I spelled it with five letters in English and in Spanish. I used language to stand for green in ways that I did not use language to enact desire. I felt that a poverty of poetry is that it requires no light or its continuous spectrum.

In her own words, Frida explained the meaning of several colors, explaining, for example, blue, green and red: "*Azul: electricidad y pureza amor*"; "*Verde: hojas, tristeza, ciencia, Alemania entera es de este color*"; "*Rojo: sangre? Pues quien sabe!*" I was transfixed, making myself as porous a receptor as I had been standing in the British Museum before the Rosetta Stone or before the Elgin's Marbles of Keats. It seemed to me that this most passionate of painters had sent to me, as I stood there in that present moment, a communiqué from the past, *un recado apasionado*, that would reveal to me the meaning of colors. For after all she was a painter: blue, green, and red were stuff that she got on her hands, made art with, and had to wash off vigorously at the end of the day: acts altogether distinct from mine as a poet who writes the names of colors.

The definition for green struck me as most odd: "Green: leaves, sadness, science, all of Germany is this color." Why? Was it true? Were science and Germany green? Sad? What, I asked myself, did it mean? These definitions sounded poetic to me, so I rationalized that since "Blue: electricity and purity love" had the ring of lyric, I should be able to make sense. But rationally, they meant next to nothing to me. I did not understand. And in truth, there is no reason that a painter's words need make sense. So I forsook understanding and resolved to react. And so I wrote the poem "Letters of Color."

Several years later, Frida Kahlo's diary was published, and once again I was struck with desire and apprehension. The diary is published as a photo reproduction, for it is the diary of an artist and is at least as visual as it is verbal. It is full of color and full of words. I turned to the page of the color definitions and found that I had been misled. The textual representation at the Mexican Museum had presented her reflections on color as if a dictionary, a list of words defined by synonym, metaphor, explanation. But in the diary, the meaning of color was something quite different. It began by zigzagged lines of two colors followed by the declaration, "*Probaré los lapices tajados al punto infinito que mire siempre adelante*," I will test the pencils sharpened to the infinite point that always looks forward. And the definitions for blue, green, and red did not begin with the words, the names of the colors, but rather began with the non-verbal blotch, sketch, and smear. There was no word red but instead a smear like a thin stain and clots followed by the words, "blood? Well, who knows!" As such, the definitions seemed to read backward, from the weak verbal explanation to the demonstration of color, from the name to blotch, from epistemology to ontology.

What I had dismissed in the Mexican Museum as disappointing writing came across in the diary as an attempt to work between media, between meaning in painting and that in poetry, between color and word. There was in the color of the blotch and smear, in the sketch of a leaf and the zigzag line, a presentation that was a thing itself along side the linguistic. In my previous reading of the definitions, I formed an understanding whose fundamental paradigm was the dictionary, which has nothing to do with painting. Seeing her diary pointed out a way that color differed from line and differed from word as well. But it was the imbrication of color, line, and word that perhaps said most. And this was as missed by my lexicographic conception as it was by the Mexican Museum display and as it is by the English translation appended to the photo-reproduced diary in color and Spanish. In our endeavors to translate, we miss the play set about by Frida Kahlo's hand.

In a dark pencil, dark gray, Frida Kahlo wrote, "*nada es negro—realmente nada*": nothing is black—nothing really. It is a clever irony for the color is in fact not black, but blackish, and more, the final nada is underlined in green. This, she tells us, is sadness, science, German. In the play of her interaction of color and word, that nothing is black is empirical, perhaps, or perhaps that nothing really is, is a sad fact. And the line "*electricidad y pureza amor*" is written in blue except for the last word, love, which is a very dark brown, the only occurrence of the color on the page. Verbally blue is defined as electricity, purity, and love, but in the play between color and word, love is set off, emphasized, perhaps as in hyperbole, perhaps as in asserting its singularity, perhaps in ambiguity. None of this is translatable in text alone, as the poor English translation so well indicates. The English spills over continuously, without the punctuation or trope of color, constructing a sadly pale verbal reading.

By seeing the graphic reproduction of the work of her hand, I came to a different sense of how she meant by color. It is ironic that I think I better expressed this sense of meaning before I saw her diary, in a poem of reaction, than I have in all these paragraphs since.

23 *echo park*

I just got off the phone with Kathleen. I haven't seen or spoken to her for a couple of years. She's producing a television show and needs some video bites about Chicano popular culture. The subject area, lucha libre, is not one of my favorites, so I recommend Harry Gamboa: he is Chicano, as smart an artist as there is, and looks good on camera. He'll do.

I haven't seen Harry in just about as much time, but we've kept in contact: failing to get money for a video project; doing photos; inquiring about the two Barbaras, his daughter's birth and his wife's health. I have known him since after he got kicked out of what was to become the premier Chicano band, Los Lobos, and formed the premier Chicano art group, Asco. I still think he has the most fertile range of any Chicano artist, though I do have to admit that I think no one on this side of the border paints murals like Willie Herron, and that's saying quite a lot. I once participated in a performance piece of Harry's and, covered with black paper, lay down on the Third Street bridge along with a lot of others similarly clad. I owe him this book, for were it not for him and the Goddess Chaos, I'd not have walked the Irish sand when I did, nor begin this work as I do. So, if I can turn him onto a brief television thing, so much the better.

The last time I saw Kathleen we got into a misunderstanding about sex. An actress friend of hers took me to visit Kathleen and Bill, her screenwriting lover. When we got to their house in Echo Park, there were others there as well, three film editors and Kathleen's assistant producer. I was the only non-Hollywood type there, and if you include wannabes, the only one in half the city as well. We ate barbecued fish and vegetables, looked out at the city from the hillside, and carried on conversation, part of which touched on the similarities between Johannesburg and Los Angeles, the segregation and gated communities, all of which was news to me, having never been to South Africa.

Eventually talk turned to violence, and Kathleen mentioned that in the course of her work she saw quite a bit of violent footage. Concerned with what I considered to be an occupational hazard, I asked if she found herself becoming desensitized. After she gave a brief and vague response, I pressed on: had, in fact, her work diminished her passion? With that question, I inadvertently crossed the lines of communication in a most entertaining way. Kathleen was taken aback by my question; Bill, indignant. What business was it of mine, he seemed to ask. I realized at that point the *passion* in Hollywood parlance is something quite different than it is among poets. I continued, pushing for a direct response even though it was clear to all that I was prying into their sex life. I think *passion* is a euphemism in cinema and television for *coitus*, and so to inquire about losing passion is to inquire about losing ability to climax. It was great fun, and we all left laughing.

Part of the magic of dance is that it resists an essential impossibility through physical acts, through real leaps of faith. As an articulation of the body in rhythm, dance coordinates movement with beat, whether up, down, or off. Beats are read as a pattern, and the body moves rhythmically in dance. The impossibility is simply that dance relies on a faith in rhythm. For while the dancer perceives rhythm as a syntax of beats, rhythm's value for dance lies in its telos, in a pattern projected into the future. Rhythm structures events that do not yet exist.

Dance rests on the projection of rhythm, the sense of which rests on the relation to, and the matter of, time. It is faith, perhaps, faith that a next beat will come to be, that allows rhythm to be realized, and that allows the body to synchronize movement with the beat in the rhythm of dance. Or if not faith, even a weak and naive one, it is physical fact, or if not actual fact, it is practical correlation, that informs the keeping of time and that inspires one's keeping on time in the series of motor and musical events.

Dance configures beats in a sense of rhythm and coordinates body movement in anticipation of rhythmic repetition, but as it does, what is its sense of time? Does the dancer, for example, experience the present instance of each beat in a passage of time, perhaps like an event that punctuates the flow of temporal matter or that moves forward on a line of time? If true and factual that time is the medium upon which rhythm is projected, then is dance, to some degree, not so much the anticipation of actual beats, but the measuring out of identical temporal fragments? Time as such then would be the medium, flow, line, or fabric upon which events, from musical beats to human births, happen. Dance in this sense would constitute movement as an analog to the flow of time and perhaps only secondarily as an expression of beat. But it is possible to consider dance in the first instance a correlation of movement to beat. Instead of rhythm defined as the organization of time, as musical theorists would have it, rhythm could be considered an organization of events, each beat an event with its own life, each its own whole. Such dance would be structured on the rhythm of events as they transpire, on the lives of whole events, which are not identical bits of perfectly parsed time. The possibility of dance would not be based on the fact, fabric and flow of time, but on the realization of events, on the occurrence of beats.

A present concern in literary criticism, once again, is the anti-Semitism of T. S. Eliot. Because of his stature and his dominance in modernist poetics, most especially in England, Eliot's prejudices are discussed and apologized for more often than are those of Ezra Pound or Henry James, for example. Eliot, the Missourian who became an "Anglo-Catholic Royalist" "more British than the British" is treated in something of the way that is Shakespeare: his stature nullifies serious accusations of anti-Semitism. It is a tautology applied to a writer essential to the canon: since he is great, he is great or, in a deductive variation, since his work is great art, it must be of great spirit. Eliot's depiction of a Bleistein or Shakespeare's of Shylock cannot be evidence of anti-Semitism, or so the logic goes.

The current reading of Eliot makes a distinction that seems to me similar to the problem of dance. Eliot can be a great artist and an anti-Semite; I find nothing in aesthetic theory or moral philosophy that precludes either. But one can take note of how one reads his anti-Semitism, whether in themes or in bits. The two extremes differ in that one emphasizes the general sense of the flow of meaning while the other emphasizes each literal event, one at a time. Those who emphasize theme read Eliot backwards, from a general meaning that explains individual events. Such a reading finds that the whole makes sense and makes sense of the constituent parts. To put it musically, the sense of rhythm makes sense of the individual beats.

On the other hand, locating Eliot's anti-Semitism first in the constitutive elements of *The Waste Land*, such as in the etymological, metaphorical, and grammatical bits, emphasizes the construction of meaning along other lines. The individual events of the text come to accrue meaning through syntax, through a logic of synecdoche and sequence. The lack of capitalizing jew or the etymology of Bleistein can be identified as fragments in the logic of Eliot's anti-Semitism, or can they? Critics of this reading of Eliot often argue that each such poetic event, on its own, is benign and can appear prejudicial only to those so predisposed to finding anti-Semitism.

In a nonpoetic example of the syntax of prejudice, the video tape of the LAPD beating of Rodney King broke down the movement of racism into its individual beats. On behalf of the police assailants, Stacey Koon and Laurence Powell, the defense attorneys slowed the video tape to its individual still frames, down to the individual events of the beating. They then challenged the jury to identify the exact instance of the violation of civil rights. The defense insisted that at no individual beat in the dance of police violence was it possible to identify a rhythm or theme of racism. After an acquittal and the LA riots, Koon and Powell were subsequently convicted of the lesser crime of denying civil rights. The defense for racist beating or anti-Semitic writing is that the individual beat need not participate in a rhythm.

In the end, it is not the passage of time or the freezing of time that matters so much in the story of a beating: each nightstick blow hurt with each individual strike, and the sequence of blows by white LAPD officers on a fallen Rodney King beat out a pattern, beat out a racist rhythm. The story of racism is a series of beatings, blow by blow in a rhythm whose theme is dominance. The dance of power, the movement of bodies to administer violence in the single beat as well as in rhythm, is a dominance that mystifies. Racism has no time. It is a pattern of beatings here.

25 *life*

Last night I drove to the Mission District to attend a benefit, and as I write this I am listening to a recording of "Desapareciones" by Los Fabulosos Cadillacs. I listen to the lyrics by Rubén Blades and recall the lyric last night by Lorna Dee Cervantes, and I write now, I know, about the end. Lorna read a poem about a very particular ending, about a moment now approaching two decades past, when San José police shot Danny Treviño, killing him as he sat unarmed in his car. Lorna's rhetorical trick brings Danny before us, alive by the will of the poem. This is what Rubén Blades does in his salsa lyrics: he bears witness and testifies and vivifies the dead by singing his canto of recollection.

The event last night was to forestall an end: the artist Yolanda López is gravely ill, and the artistic community gathered to show their love and to raise money for her treatment. A particular pallor was cast over the event because José Antonio Burciaga was unable to make the drive up from Monterey, being too consumed by his own battle with cancer. And a momentary scare for us was the news that José Montoya had had a stroke, but his appearance belied the fact: he was there to read and looked as ready as ever. Up until Ricardo Sánchez succumbed to cancer a year ago, the community of Chicano poets had not had to deal with the facts of our demise: we were all alive. In fact until Sánchez died, all the veterano poets who had given voice and form to a Chicano consciousness and to the homeland, Aztlán, were alive and writing and therefore, it seemed to us, so was the movement. Our moment of Chicano Renaissance is like the prime moments of other locations, Harlem and Paris in the 20s and 30s, Madrid and Florence in 1492.

Even though the event wasn't a funeral, it took on one aspect of the Chicano version of the death ritual: the celebration of life. We affirmed the good for Yolanda and Tony and for ourselves as well. That evening the Mission Cultural Center was the place for us to touch, dar abrazos, to catch up on the changes in our lives, and to talk, laugh, and dance. Cherrié's baby and Lorna's baby had transformed into little boys. Juan Felipe had a new book out and was going to be at Cal in the winter. Francisco had finished his series of Spanish text books. Rose was quitting San Francisco State for the life of the writer. And José was hanging in, looking bad in his tando, el mero jefe del tribu casindio. Charley, Margarita, and I chanced upon a random photo-op, having unwittingly dressed similarly: black shirts, khaki green pants.

In "Desapareciones," Rubén Blades proclaims the names and the quotidian details of life that become the frantically held links with the desaparecidos, those people kidnapped, tortured, and made to disappear by the governments in places like Guatemala and Argentina. One woman pleads for information about her husband Ernesto who was last seen wearing *camisa oscura y pantalon claro*. Someone else has spent three days searching for a sister, Altagracia, who last *salío del trabajo para la escuela*. The son of another, Agustín, is a medical student, *un buen muchacho although es aveces terco cuando opina*. In "*El padre Antonio y el monaguillo Andrés*," his song about the assassination of Bishop Romero in El Salvador, Blades details not only the life of the Bishop, but that of Andrés, the altar boy, who was killed as well, noting for example his love of soccer.

For Lorna, the telling of the murder of Danny Treviño is personal, another poem that she fashioned from a life surrounded by violence in San José's Barrio Horseshoe. Charley Trujillo responds to the poem as to another version of a familiar story. Charley writes novels about his experience in Vietnam and lectures about violence there and on the home front. He reminds me that San José police killed Danny's cousin, Tomás Treviño, as well, shooting him fifteen times as he stood in his own kitchen. Both Lorna and Charley had gone to support Yolanda, and both have been close to Tony Burciaga for a long time.

Of all the people there for Yolanda, Lorna has been my friend for the longest time. I actually met José Montoya earlier but did not get to know him for quite a while. And Juan Felipe was in my mind way, way back: when a group of Chicanos first brought Alurista out to New York, the poet of the homeland raved about this great poet back in San Diego. But I've worked with Lorna almost since I moved to San José. I remember being at San José City College and having a student tell me that this poet lived across the freeway. This was back in the days when she was working on *Mango*.

I remember when I met Lorna thinking her much like a small black bird, the kind that I'd see on my lawn. This was before *Emplumada*, and she seemed to me as fragile a creature as she was sure a poet. But after the publication of the first book she shed any real fragility and grew to something else. The end of one thing, the change to something else. A fact and trick of life.

When I came to Berkeley, three consecutive school years began marked by tragedy. In 1989 there was the 7.1 Loma Prieta earthquake: the Bay Bridge down, 62 dead. In 1991 there was the fire in the hills behind campus: 2,843 houses gone, 26 dead. In between in 1990 there was the scene at Henry's: hostages, a schizophrenic driven by voices, sexual assault, and two deaths. Henry's was one in a series of fatal fall passages for Cal students, and this in a period of trauma in a state of trauma: 6 years of drought, the LA riots, fires, floods, the

6.7 in LA, and all this besides the regular deaths by mud slides or shootings and dehydration of "aliens" lost in the desert.

My own small world had been rocked as well: divorce, a daughter's running away with a Ukrainian DJ, the break up of my family, and racism on the job front. My bid for tenure in English at Cal had turned to an ugly display of discrimination and retaliation, beginning immediately after my public reading of "Tomorrow Today," a poem criticizing the University's opposition to affirmative action. These are ugly times for Chicanos at the University of California, and victories like those of Rudy Acuña are few and extremely hard fought. Yet throughout this, it is the personal element of our struggle, the individuals who take stands as well as those who acquiesce in fear, that renders our efforts so human. It is clear to us that our struggle is not always victorious: Cecilia Burciaga, for example, was forced from her position at Stanford. The personal dimension of that struggle meant that Tony Burciaga would leave Stanford too. He was an artist-in-residence and painted the *Last Supper Chicano Heroes* mural there, but he left with his wife when she took a position in Monterey. And eventually after that, and after the moment that I began writing this piece, in another struggle in the future, cancer would kill Tony. The comic and critical poet would be gone. I have a video tape I made in 1980 of Tony and Lorna. He reads "*Letanía en caló*," and she reads "Beneath the Shadow of the Freeway." It is a testimony to the times and equally one to the spirit of the individual poets. I like the tape because it is a personal statement, theirs as well as mine, a statement to the testimony of life.

When I met my class after the killings at Henry's, I stood before the large group realizing that they looked to me to make sense of the daze. My job was to profess sense, to derive meaning from event. The place they used to meet at to drink and laugh had been turned into a place of horror by Mirdad Dashdi's insane and suicidal acts. Friends and classmates had been taken hostage, assaulted sexually, shot, and one killed. It was a particularly human violence, more personal than the earthquake the year before or the fire yet to come. I had nothing to say, almost nothing except to address the situation, to put words to the event, to bear witness and to testify in the present for the sake of our recollection. I suggested that we go and celebrate life. I did not suggest how; each student, I was sure, would have a private and personal vision. For my sake, I think it best to hold another human whom one loves.

My students left to talk with each other outside in the bright light of day. A community of Chicano poets came together for a sick artist. I have records, electronic and in memory, of testimony by Rubén Blades, Tony Burciaga, and Lorna Dee Cervantes. It is right to celebrate the living amid the killing.

Mexicans invented zero. And Mexicans were better markers of time than Europeans. In the Aztec calendar, after eighteen months of twenty days, the year ended with a vague period of five days. It was a time of chaos.

Zero time and chaos are my birthright. They are the conditions of my story, the notes of my lyric, the beats of my rhythm. I finish this book now outside numerical order, in this coda, recalling what I can just imagine.

It began during an impossibility of place, one of those instances where my daughters and I were in different times, facing different directions, and seeing in different light. I left Mireya asleep in Dublin alone on the island. I had stayed as long as I could, but the events conspired to have me leave for Italy. We had rehearsed schedules and alternative plans the evening before and had driven the Opel around in the dark to acquaint her with Connolly Station. I left early, first for London, then Milan. It was cold summer, wet.

Marisol was somewhere over North America, taking the polar route, perhaps a jet stream, east, aiming for Ireland. Her departure had changed and been changed over and over again, and neither Mireya nor I would believe that she had actually taken off until we saw her in Ireland. Xóchitl was somewhere in California. In a week she and I were to rendezvous at Heathrow and take green Aer Lingus to Dublin. These girls who mean so much to me seemed to me then like fragile balls tossed in the air at once, in flight, arcing, gliding, falling on their own beyond my sight.

Mireya met Marisol at the airport and proudly took control. The sixteen year old had a couple hundred Irish punts in her pocket and would introduce her older sister to the island and lead her to our place in Sligo. She tells me the trip went fine, the only slight mishap was taking the less comfortable train north: more smoke, less space. But this had been a conscious choice, so as to get home a bit earlier. Marisol, she says, slept the way: taxi, train, taxi. And her directions to the driver in Sligo town took them without hitch to our place by the sea, past Lissadell, between Ballyconnell and Cloughboley, at the crossroads, the fairy path, and the wild yellow irises.

While I was in Italy, they went out for a walk: I can see them. Their choices were north and west, towards Dermot and Helen's and the cliffs; west and north, toward Roskeeragh, the cold flat beach with the black slugs; south, past the well toward Ellen's; or east, past the yellow flowers toward Dunlevy's. It was warmer than it had been; they set off away from the sea, toward the farthest destination, Dunlevy's market. At the crossroads they turned left, passed the fairy path, and followed the road lined with flowers, cows, and piles of stone with the memory of homes. Eventually, after passing the slight rise a couple of miles out, they could see Ben Bulben in the horizon. The high, flat mountain was the prime marker for Co Sligo, navigationally and spiritually, but from our house it could not be seen. Its sight marked distance from home and signaled that Dunlevy's might be near.

They bought something at the market, maybe a Solero, perhaps the modeling clay, I really couldn't say, I wasn't with them. Their return, they decided, would take them past Ellen's, in a round about, alternate way. They ended up missing the turn, it being a place, after all, where the roads have no names and look similar to newly arrived urban types. They ended up at Raghly by the German castle and tried to head back in the general direction north across the fields and the bog and megaliths. For hours Ben Bulben remained visible: clearly they were nowhere near home.

What did they see then? Who had walked in the same bog millennia before? What lay buried in the preserving earth under their purview? At points across the bog, each of their steps must have been physically difficult; they must have thought themselves as lost as they were, cut off from origin and destination as well. When would their trek end, a matter of hours at most, they hoped. Beneath their feet, the bog of a small island where grew wild yellow irises, and where a well in tall bush hid somewhere not far. And in the distance were farmers and herdsmen and the detritus of a people once twice as numerous.

When Xóchitl and I did drive up days later in the Volkswagen Golf, we were greeted by a fire of coal and peat. Dermot and Helen had dropped off dried slices of the bog for us to burn. Mireya and Marisol noted the ease with which we had arrived and related the tale of a long, long walk across a bog.

Coco Fusco tells me that she is leaving for Chiapas. I tell her that as soon as I put down the last period to this thing I'm writing, I'm taking off for Guerrero. Perhaps, we muse, one of us will run into Marcos or Lucio. Our talk turns to Mexican cinema and two of our favorite icons, Tin Tan and Tongolele. Marisol, I tell Coco, at two or three years of age used to repeatedly declare, "I'm Tongolele."

One thing Chicanos have contributed to humanity is a sense of border. We walk and swim and get lost and find ourselves and make life there in zero time and chaos.

Tentli

> *Tentli—s. labio; pico de ave; hocico de animal;*
> *orilla de algo; fig. memoria, recuerdo, tira de escritura.*

Think of the mouth as port of desire,
an edge that marks thought from
sky and flight of birds. Want across
dreams recalled days after, desire itself
written like past motion in light.
Lip is edge, the border demarking in light
and in light of day, desire is that edge,
that border, trim and light. Had we but
edge equal to desire, bound by our simple
plans and steps of desire. Bound by our
binds of brave blows, destruction for
certain, mouth of such desire, mouth
of sex and the sex of sex, had we but
the motion at edge to take bright
time, brave motion, and destroy
some center in its cool repose.

Amor y caos

Antes, el día antes, habían las cosas,
horas de cosas, reglas, y máquinas.
Nací, lo sé por la lógica griega
y por el orden de la historia de hombre.
Antes, el día antes, tuve yo una vida,
debe ser, y tuve momentos, llamas
verdes, azules, y una fé, tuve fé.
¿Porqué los libros, fotos y las huellas,
sino pruebas del diccionario, sino
del paso perdido de cristo, sino
la linea quebrada que llega hasta tí?
Se dice que antes existían cosas,
la muralla de minutos, fil de horas;
un sueño lleno, dicen mis amigos,
existía antes de que te conocí.
Antes no había nada.
En tus ojos no nací aquel momento
ni en tu vista comenzó mi vida allá,
pero después, un día después, cayó
el pasado a pedazos, a pedazos.
No dudo ni creo yo:
Antes, el día antes, habían las cosas,
y antes no había nada.
En tu vista verde de caos, ando,
en tu respiro mi paso de nuevo,
en tus dedos de minutos el tiempo.
Quebrado al momento ando,
suelto de la significación, la ley,
aquí en la detalla clara de tu ser.

Driving in Fog

She breaks silent, "Asina
es perder el alma," gives voice
once. This is how it feels, driving
in fog. What time is it after all
to lose one's soul may be what
she felt but just asked, "¿Qué
horas son?" What if you run off
into the fog and I never see you
again, even as I stop and peer? What
if I want so much to touch your skin?
If the sound of heavy wind is all
we'll ever hear, if there is nothing
beyond an edge, just beyond
our sight? Does it creep into the car
interior, so diffuse up close I don't
see it fog the windshield with its
thinnest of membranes?
The point about fog is that this
muffled obfuscation is swirling, top
quarks of fog set loose, decaying, and
it matters not whether we know this,
fog is now only and will never be.
Whether gift, blessing or sign: it is fog.
It is not as the Russians believe,
not like flying diaphanous in deep air.
I am driving in fog. Where are you beside

red

Nunca nadie me podrá parar
Sólo muerto me podrán callar
Caifanes

DIVERSOS

Camino imaginado

Blue leaves, hojas rotas in the shape of stars.
Ni un "no" en tu vocabulario but for others;
blue in place of green in the shape of Spain.
Ojos the color of dirt, chocolate, coffee, time,
azules las horas, hojas de horas van y se van,
ni una palabra, ni una queja, nor broken bit
a tu lado beside me andamos walking, sí walking
caminamos caminos like these, such streets, what
city.

7/15/95 Paris

Amor, Reading Letters

En el pequeño mundo de las letras
lo posible se acuesta con la física.
Por ejemplo: fueron hojas azules
que quité de tu cabello anoche,
las mismas que hallamos en los planos
impresos del museo d'Orsay,
las cuales recogí de tu jardín.
Por eso me enamoré contigo,
ladrillo a ladrillo, beso a mirada,
muralla, beso, pájaro, pluma.
Me llamas Ulises, y regreso, regresado,
mientras tu lees o tejes o fijas.

I imagine in truth because some things I know
so well: that she reads before she sleeps, shakes
her head, dives back to the sea.

8/8/95 Berkeley

B C

Un Diálogo por Ausentes

> Not as she is, but as she fills his dreams.
> *Christina Rossetti*

CRISTÓBAL ROSALES, EL ACUARELISTA,
PENSANDO EN LA AUSENCIA, ESTUDIA LA
MANO EN LA LUZ GRIS DE LA TARDE.
La traza colorida
que me engaña ya
que has huido, florece
este lado del aliento,
fuera, en el pleno aire
del sometimiento
en la cuna del tacto.

BEATRIZ ESPINOSA DESPIERTA MÁS
TEMPRANO EN UNA MAÑANA SIN COLOR.
Un día como los demás
el mismo sol calienta los ojos
y una vez más colores y líneas comienzan a acoplar;
bestias, selvas y unas calles curiosas,
como si pudieran, me preguntarían
¿por qué no te ausentas, para qué sirve el horizonte?
Examino el músculo, el hueso y
la piel en que consistes, tú que estiras en
la mañana pálido, la mañana descolorida.

Con lápiz y pincel, hazme
en cuadro plano, suelta mi perfil
de tu paleta y enciérrame en
acuarelas claras y frías, frías
como tu brazo, como tu respiro,
al último momento antes
de despertar, cuerpo
frío.

Los dibujos significan nada,
alivian ningún dolor, gastan
el tiempo, la perspectiva
y la visión.
No nunca más te despertaré.
Quédate aquí inmóvil, atrás, pintado
por tu maña triste.

Fuera de esta casa, de este taller de cuadros,
hay un charco que veo y que estuve mirando.
Es un cuerpo de agua, se aguanta entre
zoquete y cielo. Más profundo debe estar
al medio. Me voy. Tocaré la mera orilla
fría pero transparente.

EL ACUARELISTA PONE LA MANO ENFRENTE
DEL ROSTRO Y HABLA.
Beso colorado,
pintado aquí en la mano persistes;
qué vida el color rosa
y la rosa figura
te dan.

Writing Verse in Berkeley

First, examine your hand
for just hand
draws mind to paper.
The hand is not body, not noun, an act
like spark: kinesis,
electric.

Next, watch for one day
the hand act a full 24 hours, sleep even.
Note each pause, sign of weakness,
and every excess of force, no
matter how slight.
Record its casual and reflexive
grasp as well as the objects it grasps.
Schematize its movements into
a style of movement and conclude
in the act, and this is most important—
know in the act—that push
subjects things to verse: the index
of motivation, the wave of palm,
the nail tears and scratch.

Only then, fill
hand like glove, do what you will.
By sheer will power, make
hand make verse.

Afterwords, among the poets,
keep it still: neither act nor write,
freeze hand, torso and leg.
Do not tap the floor
even absently. Yet keep the eye free,
keep free the ear, the mouth.
Clearly hear Cynthia pierce one line,
"the irony . . ." focus

on the metal *in her voice* that
can rust, can be magnetized.
For this is what is
in verse: words rust, words magnetize:
attract, repel, decay.
Recall a trick of children:

> *Four dark coins touch in line*
> *on a smooth light surface. Press down*
> *three with three fingers of your hand.*
> *Push a new coin, hit the rest,*
> *and break the last coin free.*

It can never matter how hard, nor even if, you press,
it will always fly beyond your reach.

Tomorrow Today

October 11, 1995

Tomorrow marks
five hundred and three years
since Columbus found his way
to the Americas, half
a millennium and three years
since the story of contact began,
since Europe came west.
Tomorrow marks the anniversary.
Five hundred and three winters
have transpired, as many springs,
summers, and falls. Those seasons
are gone, those times have passed,
there is nothing we can do,
they are gone.
Tomorrow we will remember
October 12th, 1492,
here in the United States,
tomorrow will be Columbus Day;
here in Berkeley,
it will be Indigenous Peoples' Day;
here in Califas, Aztlán,
it will be Día de la Raza.
As many winters have passed,
as many suns have set, as many
minutes and seconds have come
and gone, up to the same tomorrow:
Columbus Day, Indigenous Peoples' Day,
Día de la Raza;
but they are not the same.
For we are different and we mean different
when we celebrate
the discovery of a new world, imagine,
a new world, or different when we solemnize

the most severe genocide in the history
of the world, the most severe, or when
we recognize the birth of a new race,
a new race. For twenty-four hours tomorrow
we can celebrate the greatest act
of the Renaissance and the act of a single man
in Columbus Day,
and we can solemnize
the deaths of tens of millions
of Native Americans and the extermination
of whole peoples, such as those
on the islands of first contact,
remembered in Indigenous Peoples' Day
and we can
recognize miscegenation and the possibility
of contact between races
in the birth of hybrid, mestizo peoples
in the Día de la Raza.
Tomorrow is Columbus Day,
it is Indigenous Peoples' Day,
it is Día de la Raza: all exactly
mark five hundred and three years
and all exactly mark something different.
The events that have happened
in the interim have happened,
nothing can change that.
The first joy at the sight of land
happened. The unspeakable terror
of parents watching their child
fed to conquistadors' dogs happened.
Five hundred and three years of events
took place, we cannot change that.
We cannot stand up like Las Casas
and say this must stop; we cannot
tell the Tainos, on first seeing the Spanish arrive,
to run, to run, and not to stop running.
What was, was.
We cannot change the number of days, nor

can we change the events that happened.
We can, though, choose to remember or forget,
to celebrate, solemnize, recognize.

Last year
my state expressed hatred for my people
marking in law Mexicans as the common evil,
going as far as denying vaccine
so that those of us not deported, aborted,
or incarcerated, could die from childhood disease.
The majority of Anglo Americans, of African Americans,
Asian Americans, the majority of women
supported proposition 187.
Why?
Why is it that Chicanos and some Latinos
are the only people whose majority opposed it?
I am not bitter, but I do not forgive.
Don't all of us know, don't we all realize,
the terrible danger when we allow ourselves
to choose among ourselves and choose one
people for exclusion? Don't we realize
what we do to ourselves when we delude
ourselves and support a solution that marks
one people illegal? Any ultimate solution,
any ethnic cleansing, any racism,
any xenophobia of hate, hurts us all.
Each and every one.
For each small act of exclusion
opens the door for more.

This year,
the regents denied affirmative action.
Those regents who direct the university
that employs me, that educated me,
voted for exclusion.
This year, they met and they voted
to prevent Cal and UCLA,
to prevent Riverside, Irvine, and San Diego,

Santa Cruz, Santa Barbara,
Davis, and San Francisco, to prevent
this university from fair policy,
from policy that opposes the practice of exclusion,
from policy that had made opportunities
for people, including me.
Earlier this year the regents so voted.

Tomorrow, we will not be able to change
five hundred and three years of events:
Columbus did what Columbus did; whole
peoples have been exterminated, nothing can
bring them back. But tomorrow, we can
choose to remember or forget, and if to
remember, we can choose how to recall,
we can decide what all that time, all those events,
what all those acts mean.
And our act is significant.
It is true that the regents have voted,
it is true that they have struck down
affirmative action, but it is not true
that nothing can be done about it:
the matter is not over.
Each regent who voted is still alive
and more importantly, I am alive,
and more importantly still, we
are gathered tonight here and we
say the matter is not over.
Some things cannot be changed
but this can.
Whether any individual regent
voted out of intimidation by the governor,
or to support his presidential bid,
whether out of deep seated racism, or
naive misconception: it does not matter:
that vote was wrong.
I stand here now and say to you
it is wrong to impede us; any step backward

hurts us all. Those who imagine good
from a politics of exclusion delude
themselves: each selfish gain comes at
a cost to all: we share the university,
we share the state.
Affirmative action is not dead history,
sealed and written, it is a live issue
one that right now we are waging.
I stand opposed to racism,
opposed to sexism,
opposed to ethnocentrism.
I oppose the politics of exclusion.
I affirm our action.

Lebensraum

Das Gringo Volk braucht Lebensraum
for theirs is the greed of greed.
The gringo folk need living space
to bury, to bank, to breathe.
Al gringo le falta más room to live
que la avaricia puede ganar,
ciento ochenta y siete grados más
que la avaricia propia puede agarrar.
The gringo folk need more dead space
free from natives, their kids, their words,
a living space above the dead,
to capitalize on greed of greed.
Das Gringo Volk braucht Lebensraum
dead space that makes no sense,
200 million dollars saved for billions lost
to deny Mexican kids vaccine
and a place to write, to read.
The greed of greed is the law of the land
in Kalifornia, Kapital of the dead.

Prayer for the Death of the Soul

We pray for death of one soul.
One man, who may in his heart have love
for others, love for other men, for women, children.
We do not see his love and do not know
nor can know what is in his heart,
for that is known to you alone.
But his mind's work we see.
He has taken his wisdom, and bent by hate,
he has come to hate. He has come to hate
the rainbow you gave us, proof of your undying love,
and he strikes at our eyes.
His mind, so torn by fear, has come to fear
the sounds of our names, our voices,
and he strikes at our ears and tongues.
And what he does to us, he does to himself.
He claws his own skin at night and when he is alone,
he cries out because he has cut
to his very soul and killed the gift you gave.
We pray for the soul he has killed.
Deliver him from himself.
And deliver us from such hate and fear.

Net Laguna

Je voudrais dormir au bord du lac,
al lado de este que en inglés es lack,
to sleep beside lo que je voudrais,
junto al lago peut-être nager.

Je voudrais dormir in the wide aire
mentir in the cut, herida mía;
avoir des rêves al revés de anger,
rage, où nagent les anges d'argent,
rien, and rain entero peace of time.

To ask la cuna of first, ¿qué es, pez?
Passé pescado, sin essense, pecado original,
con d'ailleurs de l'essence un seul poisson,
the poison sol au bord laguna cut water
corps de l'eau, de l'heure, and the fold que eres.

Une tranche de la vie, flesh bits, minutiæ,
¿qu'a bu qui a vu qué ha visto l'año que entra quién?

Blue, Sharp, Still

is not water
or ways emptied
of dust broken black.
Curved fact of thing nothing like
sub-things and para-thing

Not at this moment, pretend at this, of gazure beneath and amid the broken stream of inanimates thriving across broad bands, not what is then agreed to as the full impression of things, pretend, the impression of matter on things that issue. Palettes before the black surface of things-in-fact shine if they could or could not lie before the issue of breakage confronting spill invented as some thing scene:

Therefore the emotion
thus rendered tangible
is by the sense of break
a whole black palette
imagined lucid
as so the start off perch
is the narrowed band
and length
and this short length
is trace only
and this sense is
that of short length
unlike another or the
midnight fire of any
para-thing's heat
and is the convergence
of angles narrowed
length and depth
and wide too terminal.
This thing of unreflected
surface and effulgent core
gives back the whole white

in silver bands of if
it had volition unchecked
or broken like the arc
is broken water.

The convergence is one that facts potential of energy in form, relying, pretend, on the real of consistency and the is of shape to incise and cleave like it does. The point of issue is its relentless, pretend, push to self, expressing in potential the plunge and thrust and narrow angle of a matter on the verge of break, the slender break, unlike the spill but near time

CARTAS

19.2.93

Escrito en agua

Se acaban los seis años de sequía
fácilmente: dedos de agua llegan
por fin a la cara seca, la cara retirada.
La casa, la camisa,
traspasada por lluvia demasiado
atenta, se convierten en líneas
de versos de bestias de selvas de hojas de papel
secas, mojadas, remojadas.
Por seis años una California sin
canto, sin ganas existía. El color de aire,
agua es algo común. Se dicen
que no existe en el desierto,
pero fíjate: hay bastante en sombra y letra
para creer en vida por toda la vida y además
para terminar una época seca, para matar
silencio en las hojas.

12.3.93

Trozos

Si *pedazo* no tiene una esencia propia
y, a la vez, es la pura verdad que
nunca alcanzaremos un cuerpo móvil
que ya ha arrancado ayer,
¿cómo podemos comunicar? A pedazos
llegaremos, tantas aguas diáfanas, cuando
la luz reteblanca se quiebra encima de
la mesa y revela a sí mismo
esencialmente: lo que es una gota o otra, es
tal trozo humano a tal fragmento
nocturnal de la ciudad, es isla
a la marea menguante:
pasos claros, ocultos, atraviesan el mar
lago, laguna, lágrima, huellas
en las pieles de un agua quebradiza,
fronteriza, traspasada no más con un cambio
de ser, una pausa al medio corriente,
hasta bruma, vapor, o humedad necia.
Claro, se trasluce y se vierte en seguida,
el blanco pedazo del sagrado blanco,
y sin esencia, enajenan todos los
fragmentos, insensibles.
¿Qué hay? ¿Qué cae?

1.4.93

Varias respuestas

La música, por ejemplo,
existe al momento.
Su recuerdo nos engaña
precisamente porque es
mentira. El dibujo que miras
después de cerrar los ojos
no se distingue mucho
de cualquier foto o pintura: es
algo visto, es algún ser. Lo que
puedes detener, parar en media
vuelta, es algo, claro, pero no es
vuelta, ni corriente, ni ritmo.
La vida, por ejemplo, cruza
líneas y nos desengaña
aunque creemos el contrario:
no es cosa, ni tiene ser.
Los versos se despiden así,
acuérdate. Los huesos se despiden
así. Tantos ecos, así.

24.4.93

La joda española

Si por muerte entendemos el sereno
y por vida entendemos lo sereno . . .
                    No.
Si está lleno el autobús de desconocidos
hasta dormidos unos
pero sé bien de dónde vengo y más o menos
a qué hora acabaré . . .
                    Mejor.
Cuando te veo de paso me pongo a dormir,
si por paso entendemos el tráfico ilegal
y por "tú" y "yo" entendimos la misma cosa . . .
                    Sí.
Largos están los caminos reales hasta la muerte
y qué pena dar una mal vuelta: a los lados, afilado,
no es hielo, es vidrio, es espejo, es nada.

29.5.93

Palabras masculinas

Mentira pura la letra,
la desesperanza, la fortaleza:
mentira pura el dios inhábil
de las tres cruces, tres veces
desocupado: mentira las nubes
que mienten y que se hacen
tales ficciones: y más mentira
el amor que arde hasta el hueso,
irradiando lo que no puede quemar.
Pura mentira pura la pureza de la
mentira más mentida. No es que no más
no creo en las letras: no
creo que existen: aquí sólo yo grito
solamente en la plena luna
"mentira." Por eso vale el sexo:
sí puede mentir pero, ¿para qué?
Si es o no es, no me importa,
lo que vale no cuenta.

19.9.93

Aparte ir

Después de la muerte del tono,
queja de la línea telefónica,
persiste el recado, son y paso
de la estructura del danzón: estampillas
despegadas con cartas blancas: qué
selvas matinales, maritales, qué danza
marginal, qué pelo negro. Así
desenmarañan nuestras piernas así,
tuya, mía, mía, tuya:
la trenza que un día nos hicimos
desenreda, y el doble hélice
que enlaza a ti y el que enlaza a mí,
día con día, también: tal como
pierna y pelo, el ADN. Aparte
te vas, me voy: la distancia
en los matorrales.

20.11.93

Rama

No hay versos en los árboles,
        pero sí hay papeles.
No hay aduanas en los romances,
        pero hay pistolas.
No hay nada que tomar en el hospital,
        no más hay tiempo.
No hay bastantes horas,
        sólo rinde el cambio.
No hay nada más que tristes monedas en la iglesia,
        mas el crucifijo.
No se halla cura en un perdido veneno,
        porque las aguas de reflexión ocupan espacio:

Cae la catedral y sube el agua a la vez
        a causa del reflejo y el ser de la superficie del lago,
        y refluyen más allá de los orígenes ocultos,
        olvidados o perdidos.

18.4.94

Coordinada

Después del abandono, traición,
desprecio, rechazo, huida, fastidio, [fatiga]
amor obsesionante, amor puro, mero y honrado,
muerte de un hijo, primer beso, carta tarde,
y el perder todos menos a ella,
permanece lo más pobre que nos da la ciencia.
Las coordinadas cartesianas localizan
cualquier cuerpo humano en el espacio:
equis, i griega y a veces, la zeta,
explican todo y nos ofrecen el consuelo
racional, que quiere decir, lo desapasionado.
Pero como llegamos a experimentar:
el cambio cambia a uno y a los dos,
el sujeto no es igual a, ni se refiere
a, su pobre yo. Nunca en ninguna vida.
El cuerpo tal como el alma no es número,
ni es el rumbo de la vida una ecuación linear.
Sólo dejamos con la probabilidad
y la estadística: ella esta aquí, casi, quizás,
ahorita, parece. Y la coordinada nada vale.

9.5.94

Cuentos impasibles

1 luna para ti.
2 soles para que te ardes para mí.
3 dedos desmochados para ti.
4 papeles blancos para mí.
5 iglesias de cartón.
6, para mí, vasos vacíos de verdad.
7 cosas perdidas, como la sombra anoche.
8 veces solo.
9 corazones de piedras verdes para ti.
10 veces tarde para mí.
11 es nada y tú lo guardas bien.
2 soles para que te ardes para mí.

7.6.94

La red

Una matriz es el abecedario,
o, por lo menos, una serie estrellada,
una actriz desafortunada, acostumbrada
a dormir sola. Me desmiente en
media locución con su mudo perder:
cae abrazo a un acto desanimado, a pedazos,
lo que fuera el acto del brazo
cae a una significación, una avaricia
del deseo sin conexión al querer.
La telenovela conecta las quejas
de Hollywood o Churrubusco
a mi genio raso, estrellado ya.
Y la ausencia del caso no es una treta
temporal, pero acaso la red se anima
el fin de los ángeles. Y en fin me quedo
preguntando, ¿por qué es femenina
la mano, es masculino el dedo, y femenina
la uña? ¿Y por qué tropiezo tanto,
sin sueño con la red?

13.7.94

Contrabando y natación

Pero, al acabar de desear,
¿cuáles aguas imaginadas?
Labios son libros en algún sentido.
Como impregnan las hojas y
se derraman las letras hasta
la significación, y eso aunque
se localizan lejos del borde de
los lagos del significado.
La mano sentida, dormida
la izquierda, frías las dos,
tratan de nadar como árboles
californios, como las manzanitas,
por ejemplo, en medio de una
niebla de comprender. Sí,
sí hay el trabajo de la boca, sí,
la pureza del tráfico nos emociona, y sí,
la encrucijada también.

SILVAS HUMANAS

Amor

Usted se halla en la ciudad
nueva, yendo por el metro, no, mejor
afuera, viajando en un tren, dejando
atrás y a la mano derecha cualquier
edificio o rascacielos inútil
a través de la ventana borrosa,
montaje y borrador, allí esperando
adelante, en tal trayecto tal hora,
el próximo pueblo, por lo cual busca
para descubrir lo que proponen el
mundo, el tren, los sentidos humanos.
Porque aquí la luz traspasa el vidrio en
planos geométricos, se da cuenta
de las naturalidades de Juan Gris
por primera vez, planos claros de un sol
ardiente más allá de la ventana
cerrada, claros planos ya adentro en el
coche del tren, banderas luminosas,
como si la luz tuviera sustancia
ondeante, navajas brillantes, como
si diera a luz la luz a un corazón que
recordaría este sueño de dormir
sólo al despertar. La luz que revela
al mundo afuera, el árbol, automóvil,
la niña jugando lejos, divulga
también, y con la misma facilidad,
las cosas del mundo dentro del coche,
en este lado del vidrio, tan fácil,
aunque es más chico el mundo móvil, mundo
hecho partículas, más frío a causa
de las leyes de física que tartan
de tamaño y temperatura óptima.
Un plano de luz tienta
la cara de ella de repente como
antagonista a ella sola, porque

para los otros pasajeros aquí en
el mundo chico, móvil, apartados,
ellos con sombreros, que fijan libro
y periódico, que hablan un poco,
fuman poco, para cada uno de ellos
la luz es cosa distinta pero no el
plano fatal de una tragedia griega
manifestado en onda y particular
en seguida, tirado por la diosa
envidiosa, feroz, exactamente
a la piel, al labio, al ojo de esta
cara distinta a los cien kilómetros
por hora ahora. Pero ¿quien va a ganar,
las fuerzas naturales, que se acercan
muy cerca a la fuerza del destino, o la
cara de una mujer que es tan humana?
Pone abajo, a su lado, en el asiento
vacío, el libro adornado con letras
y colores interesantes, y en un
movimiento gracioso se levanta
de intento y al principio comienza con la
mano izquierda, luego con las dos, jala
el visillo y vislumbra la sombra aquí en
el mundo de los sentados móviles.
Por unos kilómetros
usted se ha dado cuenta que ese libro
ruso de escritora armenia ha cambiado,
casi como si una voz incognita
articulara la palabra impresa
y la hoja encuadernada al momento de
la lectura y el toque del libro ruso, o en
otro sentido, como si se hubiera
convertido en una de esas pinturas
cubistas de dicho libro, un ejemplar
de tal europa, porque claro que sí
es Europa, fantástica por causa
de ser una sin muerte. Pero no es, es
el baile de luz y sombras, el viaje

de Dante hasta el infierno por segunda
clase, viaje a la nación del destino
se dice en el boleto, la hora, origen
y destino, el precio: luz y sombras más
y más pesadas, el ritmo más y más
lento, una música que se oye por la
primera vez, danza típica y triste
despacio van los pasos indígenas
despacio, pasos quietos, despacio más.
Alzo la pluma, cierro el
cuaderno para más fácilmente entrar
al mundo vivo y ambulante en que me hallo
también y además, para contemplar los
planos claros e invisibles de una luz
colorida en su quietud elemental
aquí en medio del mismo viaje, otro
pasajero con su reloj e imagen
de la red de paradas blanco y negro.
A ella digo pocas palabras porque
aunque falla fácilmente la lengua
y se confunden los sentidos, es más
complicado cuando ella piensa en la
tragedia griega clásica mientras lee
una novela rusa, en una rusa
armiñada, por eso digo unas
pocas palabras en un castellano
americano, el mismo que hablaría
con catalán o filipino. Pero
porque se trata de amor, yo toco la
cara de ella con los mismos dedos
con que yo detengo la pluma, pero
sin pensar en escribir, tocar hasta
ver la diferencia en temperatura
de cuerpo a cuerpo, la que significa,
según la famosa psicoanalista
francesa, el abismo horrible y el nocturno
opaco, que nunca se desvía aunque
los hombres han construido tantos puentes

patriarcas encima de la marea y el
arroyo, sobre la ola, sobre el hoyo.
Usted nos mira y usted
se arrima a nosotros despacio, poco
a poco con movimientos de un ave
terrenal, y oye un fragmento, fragmento
de verso, como un trozo de un bolero
pero una canción sin guitarra o cuatro,
sin melodía, unos fragmentos rotos
literalmente de las planas claras,
oye cuando traspasan el vidrio que
aparta mas que contiene este libro y
detiene en su ser un mundo más de su
visión de su ser, trasoye algo breve
entre las vocales 'a' y 'o'. Y usted se halla a
sí mismo en la cama en la noche oscura
y tiene los ojos abiertos pero
se ve nada, literalmente nada,
y puede imaginarse sin límite en
cualquier parte siquiera ahí donde los
sentidos humanos no pueden mostrar
lo contrario, una liberación pura,
y recuerda la música de voces
y la temperatura de una piel en
la plena luz del sol, más o menos al
mediodía, móviles. Sabe que este es
el amor, nadie puede decir más o
explicar lo que ocurre en su ser: amor
es una palabra de dos sílabas
está hablado en dos voces en seguida
en planos invisibles pero claros,
móvil y con alta temperatura.

Sexo

El alfabeto del sexo emprende equis
y que esa x es la primera letra,
la escritura manifiesta así lo que es:
los enloquecidos símbolos se creen
criaturas vivas aunque no lo sean,
se hacen genitales, se hacen figuras.
La vagina deletrea con x
«exacto es el son de la venadita,
benditos sean todos los animales
que con genitales están escritos»
deletreada con *X*.
La verga es otra cosa, analfabeta,
letrada en la equis de unas mil penas:
pieles blancas enviadas como cartas
postales, o correo electrónico,
cuya ontología tan dudosa está.
California es el sitio sexual, frío,
y mentiras son las otras historias
contadas por unas líneas celosas,
tan lejos de noche y la red de nada
que algo sexual no tiene una pareja.
La ciudad, Los Angeles,
Este lado cogiendo descuidado,
los cuerpos de las letras se desbordan,
equis vaginas con rayas borradas,
borrachas con rayas las vergas *X*.
Desconocido pueblo de las horas
de los días de las pieles ocultas,
visibles momentos en ecos de pies
actuales en los caracteres negros,
en los textos carnales anónimos,
conocidos, y ellos bien deletreados,
porque equis comienza el acto del sexo,
germina la cadena de las letras
en ambas la verga y la vagina
de Los Angeles, ahí en el lado Este.

El sexo aquí articula
tan noche el lado este, tan bestial, penal,
se penetra el acto de sentido ante
el animalado acto de hacer letras:
la equis no vale no más ni por su alma
y se convierte en símbolos bestiales;
de las dos líneas, una permanece
virginal como un pinto deshuevado,
pero al otro lado, la otra línea no
simula lo que fue, un más manso perro,
sorpresa, en cambio, la otra se deslía,
línea, como monja desarreglada,
se derrama del orden de la raya:
línea se convierte en letras, C y S.
¿Cómo se escribe el sexo?
Sé ese modo de animar, como animan
los animales alfabetizados,
C línea S, verga cruza vagina,
rosa raya aguacate, equis ausente.
Cruzada, sin preferencia, la gata
negra no halla en la muerte ni en la raya
C y S ni una diferencia oculta,
ni misterio ante la letra o la otra:
negra es la noche negra,
negra la falda de la noche negra,
también sombra en la isla nocturna, sombra,
negro aire de piel nocturna, rayada,
gris tras negro tras gris tras negro tras gris,
equis línea sexo, equis C y S,
tras la negra faja de la noche tras
el movimiento de la negra gata
que es la danza sexual de la estampa equis,
que es el ánima de la huella C y S:
Sí, las cruces emprenden el sexo aquí,
el acto nos hace y nos hace al revés,
el equis gato es la gatita negra,
sombras gruesas y caracteres negros
en las blancas sábanas y brillantes
caminantes que cruzan la calle ancha
antojándose la negra letra equis.

Muerte

Hágase el corazón una inglaterra:
ínsula, pequeña, baja. Hágase
cambiar el ritmo: deje atrás el pulso;
goce una lluvia débil, incesante,
y baje todas las temperaturas,
incluyendo grados y pulmonías
de los poetas románticos, cada una.
Hágase el corazón un imperio, sí
con heráldica, herederos y herencia,
con una línea real, verde y húmeda,
honrosa aunque asquerosa. La bandera
debe estar verde y mojado todo hasta
la chispa. La música también debe
sembrar las lágrimas de vez en cuando.
Olvídese de las penas porque aquí
todo es lo mismo: estará cansado
al despertar tal como al subir pisos.
Además, los libros cuestan bastante
y los autores escriben bastantes
versos. No dura mucho tiempo para
aprender a tomar café mudado,
café de hierba fresca y fragante, y no más
estará un poco más difícil para
entender las reglas de las fragancias,
y todo huele bastante. La reina
no será su amiga, no se lo olvide,
le tratará de irlandés, pero puede
declamar unas escenas teatrales
ella sin equivocación, ¡que viva!
Hágase el cuerpo un papel. Cada día
escríbame algo triste y mándeme la
voluntad por las manos o el vello de
la mejilla. No se olvide de traer
lápices, las computadoras están
superfluas, acuérdese. Verdes, las

corrientes corren hasta los fines de
la insulita: corra también hasta tal
filo. Hágase el corazón ladrillo,
hinque la rodilla a la hora de albañil.

LOVE IN THE TIME OF AFTERSHOCKS

6.7

I Absence, the First Instance

Loss, as in love, the pause, respite, moment of interval between breaths, inhale, exhale, the moment of pause: think for a moment, is the stop at lung's fill or lack? Yes, the pause in the rhythm of motion of air, a life, one could imagine, in the in between of air motion, and the wait, of the very being, the wait of the air, the supporting ether of flight, the wait of wings, diaphanous angels, the breath of wings of that stop that enables the rhyme of flight, the wings of angels: Stopped, just then, we are sure, we are all sure, city of angels, of wings, and breaths, and air moving, flight suspended, just then, an interval of the silent and sure of the very breath of the angels, of the city of my birth, the city that infused me life that wrote me *in spiritus*, just then, in the in between of my very breath, moment mine, interval I breathe between just then. It is like that space between beats: within the gap of systole and diastole, of heart like drum, between the down and the up of beat, just then, caught in arrest, mid beat, unsure of the dance, of the very rhythm itself mid flight. So it is as it seems if sight is an arrow and the city of angels lags from its flight, it is just so: wait a motion and it has passed, silent and slight air, see it is so, city mine. Just then in the pause and in the empty break, arbiter of difference, in the lag and gap and stop mid flow: it is as it seems, mid flight amid the flap of wings of angels in flight in the city at night. So it means this and this is what is seen if what just then is taken for real, if the blank of the clock while we inhale or ex is taken as time, as the moment to which it refers, and thus we mean what we separate: this from that, in from out, flight from night, diaphanous flight of mine. Night and the absence of night as its negative, black and the absence of blank as its clone, and time in shard we cannot gather nor hold but watch pierce our palms in the shade mid day, just then but at night in the city of flight and the flight angelic of the city of night and pause and silent flow of light air like so much breath of the dead, the angelic, the holy, all in so much faint air motion beatified, just then and it is not, it is gone, if that can be a present, a gift of time, as in the impossible moment we note just then in the night city between the halves of the beat that rewrites our being in so significant and so real movements of life making, as in a pause to sigh and finding meaning in its envisioning. So? It is so, for it can be no other way if to be other is denied strictly on temporal non parallelism grounds like the way space is so cleverly impossible to afford the ambiguous, one means what one is, facilely and blind like. It is not precisely because it is: city of angel night, in flight solo.

11 *The Inefficiency of Sleep*

Off Beverly Blvd the sense of one woman alone in sleep as if an art, a script of death perhaps, for this is Hollywood and love is all it seems in an act or two, the sense not unlike absence but not that final awe, rather more the innocent murder of hearts, one in line after the next, fresh blood in the sense of solitude and the alone of the mammal in hunt: so silent in tracks across snow if there ever would be such in this city, this place of such sense, where image and sleep conflict in the light of day, in the contact with spoken Spanish on the broad streets and the traffic of humans waiting change for some better, a solitude, cruel in its purity, simplicity, and its fine atonement like sacrament by script and brief and fleeting sight: but such is the hard solitude of the image as commodity and the shadow it tracks across the snow, if such could be, of the emotional city's range. She knows 6.7 as the imprint in the space of her heart, beneath an indifferent breast left and pale nipple, there in the inner enclave there is nothing left that can be imagined by any string of practiced words, nothing of so severe a number, one that so cuts the organs of emotion, nothing like absence, like patch over well, so buried in the lack can be imagined by the single foe in the sharp guise of the lover, subject to the unwanted arrow of desire, to wide eros, and the blatant and stupid move, so like so much unseen dumb air. 6.7 marks her, scent like, beneath the gloss of skin in the light of camera and the DNA house that breathes and beats her into existence at every instant: but if we can imagine, can extrapolate the shard of instant, the interval between the beats of life, into a stretched and extended span, from mid beat to slice of day, night actually, of sleep in solitude, then such number and such genetic code mark her, her personal scent of chosen fragrance and secret body, then mark in the night of solitary sleeping, alone and unwilling to utter anything other than *no* in the course of so solitary a sleep: this is the trick of Hollywood: there is nothing beneath the gloss because it truly cannot control time except by illusion, where it lives and words, so the gloss is the meaning, the string of words are to be executed and nothing more, at the cessation of lights, all go home, but there is no home, just place, just one then for solitary sleep, for sleeping alone like a film can beside so many others or not, but self contained and hermetic, with a cleanliness born of its sad inefficiency: so alone it need invent language at every instant if it is to confirm its solitary self, unable in the loneliness of the dumb sleep to reach to the lover as subject of words and words as subject of language itself as a shared medium. Thus the inefficiency of it all. It is so much easier to hurt alone, to fling arrows to true targets and to sleep dumb and refuse to have to make up words at every instant, than to hold one other: this is the lesson of a city so born in the image of video, in motion represented by magnetic particle arrangements on long ribbons of place. *No* is the only carry over in the scene of the solitary and absent, so there is no recourse for the sad angel's breast left exposed, a pre-perspective painting, the verso of icon. An inefficient sleep follows inefficient sleep and solitude accumulates like so many leavings or wrinkles of sad age or lessons of life learned and unlearned because we live in time, such a sad inefficient opportunity left blank, a moment of nothing perfected to a lifestyle performed for the dream of a camera obscura that follows after the lights have ceased and the crew gone, imagined to carry over to the sleep of the real, from the imagined reel, to the performance of solitary sleep: what position? what fare? what dumb show?

111 *Cognizance*

The sense of motion is natural, as if truth, our skins, membranes that withhold our fluid bodies from an exterior of aridity, of spill, of infection, of change as desiccation or decomposition or at the least from what we enjoy. But the attendant sense of dislocation defies the law of the single whole, when played out a *here* is never again except as a permanence of *there* or a so fleeting *near here* as to incite wonder. And so he wakes, first of all wet, covered in the sweats of the impervious image, recalling and calling to her as if she could share the space in the now. Wakes clear headed sure of the failure of the imaging sense, fully sure of how its meaning tracks without fear as if in hunt of some vital organ for transplant and transport to the first world country, in that manner she causes the sensation of waking just then as the trace of the faint trail, cold now as it has been for so long, nevertheless incites the hunter in that logical convolution where the hunter identifies and then becomes the one hunted: at this point it happens; this, the lesson: a number is so much, it cannot paint absence. Because space is always space between, being nothing without definition, an edge, boundaries, that act always confirms state. The *of what* remains a question in the deep dark of morning before the sun and before any hint of natural life, the *of what* that is cause, even in momentary oscillation from the effect, that is truly the object and subject of the physical articulation, like perspiration just then, the question so like a *the* after sensing an echo, physically imprinted momentarily on the auditory organ, beyond the actual hearing, after the spent sound, but the plain physical affect of its former presence. And just as easily the what slides into who, even if resisting a bit the further slide to whom, and the question evolves from the abject site of distant truth to the palpable matter of a skin, a scent of hair, a flash of color shot by a breeze or shake of head: the images awaken sharp like any but the most devastating earthquakes, as if "beyond image," as the French say, like her touch for real. For who is one body. In that sharp shake awake, the slap of light from so lost a deep darkness, she in image brings him into cognizance as if into being itself, the who so importantly effecting a whom into a who in a play of subject and object and the dance of light and scent. So what was prior, in the dreamless sleep in the absent light, in the black womb that does not exist beyond simple myth, in the dead of time itself? Dead as in rock, glass, clock, tide. Wake as in beyond death, a ritual perhaps.

Take life as a gift. To possess it at the present moment in the city of the angels is better than any other she could quickly name off hand. In City Terrace at this very moment there are birds making sound; they flit from perch in the tall bush and hedge amid petals the color of flushed skin, some wine, and the rare cut of ripe nectarine. This she knows will never pass again and she is witness to a singularity: it is enough to surpass the need for sex, enough in a true way, so die just then and have fully realized the stuff of living, completely. So she inhales just then like no other human ever has and holds for a split powerful atoms of air, the very keys to life, and peers out the curved window in Lomas, terrace to the city of angels. It is a gift she gives herself: she knows and touches her forearm with three fingers of her left hand, slow, in the manner that would excite him, so simple, were he here and awake, both at the same time, this once. To touch oneself is so much more than plane confirmation, it is, rather, the impossibility of the gift, at once inconsequential and of great consequence. She exhales and disperses that particular peace of air, having tasted its use, having made it function, and having done so, sent it to plant, to tree most of all she hopes. To imagine ends because of simple transition is plain logic she knows, poor in its waste and wide in its aim, and therefore resists the definition of origin and of end, rejects etiology as a disease in itself. She takes light and warms, breathes and hears birds who use air like stair, like slide, like piece of thing, and grateful for the present precisely because it incarnates undefined by an imaginary what was and an oppressive will be. "City Terrace." And just as easily it is a fear, loose and without referent, no cause in its present wrappings, just as easily a fear like heights or open spaces or some strange insect: she is after all in so dry a place on the planet, rain it seems is never more than a memory which is a dream which is a lie which is dead anyway. Before she reaches her near wrist, she finds wonder in an apprehension, so silent, colorless and pale, very unlike skin, more like air in cough and draft: it is a fear and a means to fear, boundless in its awe on an unbordered field of play dislocated like flight. Just then. Lomas is the negation of the valley and all. In the undulations of surface taken for still in the moment of present, as present, fluctuations in space, so that up and down simultaneously are beside one another: that is Lomas, sheets of curved space, a surface that fights you and holds you and sets you up, she knows, like the valley but its negation, in affirmation of sky instead of the valley's emulation of hell and tectonic underpinnings, the *semper obscura* of the beneath and core. Simple, she believes in her simple act of taking in air and expelling air in rhythm she is making life in a progressive tense, in an idealization of invisible air, a palpable, sensible body of body. If fear is a gift in time, dead time, across a still undulation of curved space, and if too, an affirmation of ritual as in the dance of the olfactory when confronting the magic of flight, then the gift of life holds out the promise of affirmation as so much petal of color before a casual stop of bird: not more, as in the spill of hours and the desiccation of them as well, some aloe scent trick. She hears the sounds of birds, close to perceiving the birds themselves. Birds, air, petals, skin, alive in the present of the gift.

V *What Is Taken in Sex*

Streets do meet, for example the boulevards Santa Monica and Wilshire or Santa Monica and Sunset meet and cross in different zones in the site of the angels. Do on the Westside, a site of diasporic New York and do on the other, a Sunset of Spanish, stubborn resistance to bear flags and grizzly extinction. People do too. The clearest metaphor is sex in its sense of the act, motion and conflation, and in its sense of procreation, as the killing of death and stifling hour. Near the cross of Sunset and Santa Monica, in Echo Park and in Silverlake, two people wait in separate houses simultaneously thinking of each other at the same time wondering if procreation had begun at recent coupling, in the exchange of body scent and the pressure and motion of intimate touch. It was five days after Santa Monica freeway collapse at La Cienega beside the Kaiser Hospital where each, unknown to the other, took plus and minus tests in the modern fear from intimacy that scores so much contemporary energy. But sex as a metaphor is a weak lie. At best. For to envision anything that is not sex as sex is the so transparent a strategy as to delight no one except practitioners of psychology and religion. It is rather, as in is, as cuts sense or contracts meaning or best of all abuts connection, a metonym. His house in Echo Park, half way between the lake and Alvarado, up a poor hill, is in a profound sense an intermediary link between his body and the violent number of just a week past, that is, house as metonym for him and for the earthquake. But in the sharp and sudden and over before it is conceived essence of the large number, there is the echo's tale that lingers, that is nothing in that it is not, but that inspires meaning for the five days later aftershock, so well timed in the act of sex, the very act that might signal his procreation if waiting so proves. House tying self and tectonic shift in metonymy, which otherwise might be construed as metaphor of himself and the earthquake or worst, of orgasm and the earth shake into a natural orgasm. Hers is in Silverlake near a park, creased beside another hill, close as bird, connected by Sunset as boulevard and as transitory view of magenta smog display from respective front, flat windows at each birth of night across the city of night. Her name is monosyllabic, consonantal, a fact that fought her blind until she moved to the locus of epicenters beside the far coast, and for the first time in a city of vowels, appended her name and acquired an unexpected measure of peace. Which now in the expectation of shock is a diminished peace, one scratched and worn, insufficient to the demands of life in the present. Coupled at the instant five days after the 6.7 in a violent heave of ground and groan, cry, of her house walls, windows, and stuff, she grabbed for him to pull him even closer than sex can unite two, and dug her nails and pulled eight tracks of scratch across his insensate back, almost as if to recount and arouse the matter of fear itself. It is the period of wait that the ether pervades, the heavy pressure measured in atmospheres of the period of wait, in tension, apprehension, desire and anxiety. Her house is redolent with passion, everywhere signs of activity: long cracks emerge from nowhere on walls and dive towards joints, there must still be sharp bits of glass everywhere, from mirror and glass and the sole deco cat that crashed, invisible and heckling shards recanting. And beyond semen, it is perhaps the ubiquity of fertilization itself that so writes each room with the smell of skin and the narration how people are made. After so telling a tectonic clash, other shocks will follow; of this there can be no doubt: she knows and waits and crosses days off calendars as if numbers meant anything more than a fabrication by men to underwrite pain. So they measure distance: he from Echo Park to a womb in doubt, she from Silverlake to a genital of liquid, from aural retort to shards of yet indeterminant weight. Metonym is measured from metonym in a mediation of pretense, in a pregnant span of something both spatial and temporal, kinesis and spiritus, man as fluid, woman as fluid. It is an unbearable wait, without end because so pervasive even as to cut sleep, like adulterated drug, impure and fooling only those who desire. So much in number as if number were life, so much in sequence, in order, in link and line: an aftershock is like an echo, awaited, but a new quake again, like a human born, a period of heavy wait in a present of perpetual acuity, awake in apprehension even in sleep, counting off so many dead numbers, life consequence chaos.

VI *Acting Sex*

In this city, sex followed the automobile; it was an, albeit necessary, afterthought. Orgasm here is literally the consequence of a sex drive. In the time of aftershocks nothing stops: that the Santa Monica freeway is down stops no one: people fuck in vans defiantly flaunt before angels in awesome free flight. One couple does from Atlantic Blvd down Whittier Blvd, Sixth Street, Wilshire, and Santa Monica, in a rough straight line to the Pacific Coast Highway and the ocean itself: in an act of ritual creation from ocean to ocean. They recognize their small human irony—he, from the Pacific edge of the continent lives just off Atlantic Blvd, and she, from the right coast, lives in Venice, just off the Pacific. They drive holding each other's genitals like keys to the wonder of the times, and in motion at Main and Hill, they capture the aftershock: something is confirmed: at the very least a statement of existence, at the most, a deification. For this couple consumption must always follow copulation and find the greatest distance from his ancestral cuisine and hers in a simulacrum of Africa, just blocks from the aftershock. Their economy is simple: friction requires fructose.

Acts and is late (than capitalism, or postmodernism), and before asks, he recalls the lyric and fashions the request to "crash" at her place rather than, being "in no shape for driving," return to San Fernando; they could tomorrow find together Ritchie Valens's grave and visit the adobe mission all as they stop by his place to gather his stuff, and maybe, if the bent for morbidity and vacuous voyeur leaves her, check out Cal State Northridge, to bear witness to almost 7 with all senses turned up full. Her place in Whittier is her place, marked so by a crisscrossing across every square foot, by small regular print on long sheets of paper, by menageries of things, the origin of each of which she could recite like water, and by the mantle of confidence she takes on within its confines: fence, street, hedge, walls, particular light, familiar processions of clouds pausing en route to La Puente. Of course it is no, but there is no rush for each such occasion affords the opportunity to perform, and it is the delivery that, after all, is what truly communicates: there is no and there is no, and neither can touch the other in shimmer, sheen or affect. This could be and so is the occasion to extrapolate, not only could he not stay, but, why not, their trip to Ensenada was off. So in the wait for timing in the formation of posture, nature interrupts with an aftershock, it being after all, January 22 exactly p.m., and it is an event and a moment, expected in hard anticipation for this is the term of aftershocks: an interim of sensory arousal, a reason for sexual acts, for the rite of remaking the human race, for making life in a physical way from the writhing moans and sudden shaking of two coupled as if outside time, "beyond being" as the Russians say, or "beyond life" as the Québecoise poet bemoaned a life truncated all too soon, absence as the telos of cold a juncture among three rivers. But *no* is an affirmation taking loose time and slapping an order to dis the shaking earth, a move bearable only on solid ground, far from the bleeding tectonics, where lack of motion gives birth to both flippant and careless abandon and unbearable levity that is otherwise meted out fluidly between two people engaged in sex and born on the rim, tentatively. That is in a move that bases its trajectory on absolute mass and firmness of spirit, one that can therefore assume action as if on a flat and immobile place where the dance of the self is all that truly orchestrates any meaning from the solitary motion in the still and near dead site. Or stage, if you will, as in transitory feat, locating realization in daily increment, a stage for working out the hectic pace and consequent effects of being, where on stage supersedes at in the fact of self articulation, as that born of stone and bedrock where negation is a proprietary impulse as much as the reel limits of stage, her stage, as in state of being, no, in the here, no. The act of agency, the agent's act, just at the actor's agent, delimiting the walls of hours of potential within the confines of so lighted a state and stage of being: in the bright light and systole/diastole music of any auditor's ah, any moment of pure reception, taken from the actor as pure light, transparent truth, and negation of blurring of lines. No, nothing in any country. No, never.

VIII *Instance, the First Loss*

This then is the some of the moments collected involuntarily in frantic instances of wide sensory receptivity: the recollection of a cruise down Whittier Blvd may be broken into image pieces of sensory data, of sense of youth, of the only gloss of Tudi's pearl white, 13 coat lacquer off the long and at times dancing hood, may be so in a defiant rush to individuate and to, by the law of opposites, the trick of irony, valorize what it ostensibly occludes, that is, offer flash of scene and sense in a disguise masquerade decoy cover from the awful fact of order and that of unforgiving sequence. There is the sense that any drive down Whittier, regardless how imagined, must in reality proceed according to fashion, which is after all an order, that posits, as base structure, that motion must have direction, sequence, and singular occupation of transitory space. The recollection of broken sensations, of images tossed vividly, is so much a lie, one constructed to imbue subject matter, that is, to locate a fleeting present, with meaning, tautologically meaningful because it is so, and further a lie because the comfort of the truth is a well sealed casket in black peat and damp. For at base, the cruise down Whittier is as governed a flight across the Santa Monica to the San Diego at night after sex, as cast as left turn from Hill onto Main admiring the huge glass window of the cafe, as the sequence from first, in a non-numerical sense, to second and on to last. In truth the infinity from zero to one is never transversed because we are never allotted nothing zero, never face the awful lacuna and lake of difference, but are set so deceptively in motion from the first swimming of crazed sperm and the slow dance of proud ovum: and in this simple sequence of events, it is the truth and reality of the unavoidable sequence of event-ness that we may try to obfuscate with color and rhyme and the trick of art, psychosis, orgasm, fear, love. This is the awful lesson and state of being of the instances of the aftershock: 6.7 is done, written into memory like fire so abruptly that we could observe the finality of everything, but done nonetheless, but the months agonize afterwards, agon, and we live alive heightened to defy what is to follow: and what is to follow is a truth and a reality we have no business to restrict, for it ignores our significance so much like a wounded god or aborted goddess. We can defy precisely because of insignificance, small waves or particles, of density and length too small to effect. And so we prescribe the only trick that works, the act that makes humans, the act that sets up the impossible synchronization of two bodies in motion, that writes as subject the stuff that is the very line itself; an act so sacred it is abandon itself. After 6.7 at the site of angels, in the city of night, sex is an act of defiant passion, a moment of intensity that unwrites the instance-ness of raw sensing nerve endings, rewrites act itself with agency and a drive toward the sea. In the Time of Aftershocks, love is the sex of the act, is the act performed in the sight of the angels, defiant before the gods, before nature, coupling in the city of night, in the bare and awful span.

frøzen
accident

1/3: DERRIDA AND WITTGENSTEIN

1 *Frozen-like Accident*

"yet," you say zero
more of ciphers
the font being 2 full

figures mark
how natural sign bleeds
colors tear spread loose
zero by drop 1
"finger was stained"
like virgin image
how rhythm of cold water
becomes areola light
and again

2 *Red Zero*

yellow more "red"
than extreme
absent the
math

of color
blood gradient, an
arc flesh flushed
hunger rings from night
perhaps "deictic wine marks"
and seemless gradient
conform to spill
across long wave
pure, blind
and spirit

3 *One Extreme*

You envision "hair"
breadths of moment
before the rest
and consonance of
dihydrous oxide

which "could be ink"
if color were
graded tears but
no, nothing never
happens first, 4
its not really it
till its accounted 4

4 *New Euros*

Change "persists
in" this French
etymology erase
the point
erase the prior

point "directed"
from an image wholly
fair before
1's own eros

5 *Final Exit*

"Memory tracks"
the train
thought to reach
the German terminal

"away & out"
distant vision distant
phonic and scope
each falls back
upon its only course

the sign exit
exit and sortie
nullified
sortie and exit
excited corpse

6 *EndZ1*

the letters B through Y
"mere hemoglobin"
river between font
faded A, source A,
and no exit Z,
sortie teleology
perspective
perfect

"from icon red"
vanishing beyond
infraredolent point
A, beyond ultraviolent
point B, facing
Xclusive distance

7 *Schema*

"synaptic rust" is itself
trust pathos causeway,
incidental fax and
fixed set of wound,
is history

is rapture
"originals in" matters
given to procreate
in his image
know history
so it can be repeated

8 *Mist*

Simply put is
"radiant where"
seeming rays radiate
and body temperature
phonemes reach
4 more zero
yet reach
but reaching

"heat and" motion
expiate nothing
pointed 2 surpasses
reception
reflection
or refraction
pointing to all
misses nothing

9 *Areola*

The imagined
"finger was stained"
glass, the eye scene
a mirror, cold water
marks syntactile skin
terminates any out
of line work

"yet" a paraphrase
gained, tense taut
and stable for life
1 clean parallel:
a distant lost rapture
not quite first
a last stop final destination
X itself

2/3: NEZAHUALCOYOTL IN MICTLAN

10 *Red*

FIELD

Take the interior of zero
soft fleshy palpable
no, an interior from which
to radiate original syntheses,

cardinal points the navel
of locus, one circle around
the topos of field and grid
complete geometries, and the slight

slight curve of calculus,
1 whole zero offering up
proof of god in its fact
between water and between the waters

a red sky, blackish, blacker
long degrees 122
and yellow, pale, toward white
white, 37 levels,

white, the peninsula of St. Francis
a plate of peace, one cape,
the birth of island, more yellow
still, there, 1 red, more absent,

blacker, across 1 yellow breeding
presence, broken brilliant
blank after blank: 1 whole
zero, catholic its immaculate

cipher, first synthesis, origin
of encircled sign completes
the ring of god and some
San Francisco May day

primavera of the cross, of those
colors: the north and west axis
of the absent presence, white
and across, black, the east

ern sky is red, blushed rage
across black aiming long
waves toward none, a rage of
music given body in the reach

of light, the mountain range
the bay, the long river, the foothills,
it is life spilled, seens
of painted life alive

there in the color break,
San Francisco meridian May
primavera, life as in alife:
the air hard blue,

fog parts fold to bay,
a keen edged daylight strikes
glare, incises clean against
blue, pieces of painted

lives commence color,
the sound of metal strain, the
spikes of brain activity and
the polylogue of tint, tone and

shade, there, the convergence of
levels, acts and cardinals,
exactly radiant, pointing to all
not absent like conjoined heavy air

and light bent through water,
born there ocean bay and
urine, the junction of thing,
facts image beyond the

capacity of inks, the red
and black, to imagine life in
center, whole and complete,
inside the cipher the origin

alias but not really, know
ledge at the tip of peninsularity
is only half Euro terminus,
only half capital terminate,

only half endzone cochineal:
Wartezeit für mich, bitte

FREEZING POINT

The point is plain: a unitary
identity less hole than field
of flags, colors flat
on cardinal grid less

solitary than ratio of axes,
than right lengths at right widths,
where it acts an episteme
and facts apparent, joy

in the shape of human surface,
a machine transforms energy,
a field of organic intellectual,
a collection of items from youth,

a busy intersection, a museum
near the metro, a red bridge
blind to ocean, and the people
you've known. The point thus given

body there, May day primavera,
everything pointed to in arcs
from efulgent core each ray
illuminates some trace fact

scene there, the point not one
but zero corporeal irradiates
from there, each present pointed to,
in a sense named, even if ignored,

all and every shined upon,
around corners, in dream, in long waves
of light eros quiver.
There are the points: San Francisco,

a glass of water, a digit stained.

11 *Yellow*

BLOOD SITE

I, Nezahualcoyotl, poet of Texcoco,
born in the year 1-Rabbit,
son of Ixtlilxochitl and of Matlalcihuatzin,
grandson of Huitzilihuitl the Mexica,

in 4-Rabbit, my sixteenth year,
have seen the yellow earth
home, bright dirt, the bright sky,
bright flower of yellow Texcoco,

cover in red, the deep red
changing black, the color
of my father's blood, in his blood
let from his incise flesh, the red

zero of his life zero
at the hand, in acts of assassins,
men and night edge flint
blood tracks, until my father

changed to body only flesh,
a trail of cipher red,
before the near and beside,
dead Ixtlilxochitl, father mine,

voice and spirit of Texcoco,
I have seen you die.

CANTO OF FLIGHT

Flowers wither and sound
brittle things break, floral
cries pitch rage
again in short wave

and out, an image venadita:
one small deer painted
cripple, each small leg
pierced eros such anima,

such gesture could come to pass
2: black orchids and the small
red mammal fade
from sense, wither and dry

blood spurts, and the grave
tremors disappear from site,
¿adónde van los desaparecidos?
Only in song am I answered
only in song may I see them
still, bright flower
and singing painted deer
cross river points,

en el agua y en los matorrales.
Equis, the tlahcuiloco, acts,
gives lyric, presence to the fall
of father, to the fall of mother deer,

presence to the hummingbird past,
the lyric petals beating
like hooves brings life again
before me those as if alive,

Equis, Tochihuitzin Coyolchiuhqui,
gives pitch to the red and to the black,
the inks that draw life
from the dead, gives rhythm

to the flight of green birds
in lyric of absence somehow full
and complete, pregnant, flush,
his lyrics tear my home past,

make me change, take flight, leave
the home of souls who stood
beside me and will never be,

song of flight: Run cholo run,
to the island causeways impermanent,
flee to the island hummingbird,
to cactus, from yellow home

made red, changed black, go
to an island half mine, become
the cipher painted in inks
over yellow. BB = 2 flee.

MOTION

Heart beat is never twice
river, the image font
a dream wood of liquid
form in the site of dead

souls, the lyrics follow blood
points, life edge words
shape to melody, to beat

of heart like flight of the small.
I am not the man who was.
I, Nezahualcoyotl, take
flight in the graphite river,

change place for life,
leave for an island and beyond.
Run cholo run, flee
the red reach and night.

12 *Black*

IN XOCHITL IN CUICATL

Lyric points me to the end
of greed, where yellow earth
holds stem and petal all hours,
where yellow and green transform

clean to blue and to fluid
wave of earth and sky,
the lyric points away
from yellow Texcoco Xopan,

to an island cross blue,
only in lyric lies
this meaning, the only truths
in fluid: true, the world fades,

blackens where blood springs
and opens where I must face
truly, an island half mine
and there find way beyond,

to the place of flags, a pale dog,
last stop for meaning, to Mictlan,
realm of dead souls, laws,
stories where meanings reside.

ISLA NEGRA

I face the night before me
as sung in floricanto and seen
in perfect inks: I strain
in the clean night zero

to see an island amid waves
of black water, an image, a man
comes to view and as space
halves, one man, one boat.

Gato takes shape before me,
speaks: I will change your home,
board the boat, for ahead
lie the night and island, half home,

final exit for the dead. His words
faint songs, his motions precise,
we board the boat and he pushes off
silent, effortless, we glide

over black ripples, before us
island and black city etch
cold against night sky,
the waters beneath us strewn

here and again with petals,
orchids and magnolia, the water
churns and moans low as we cross,
sad moans and those of dolor,

as if petals were faces watching
my flight. We strike earth
and debark to black earth and sky,
Gato leaves and I follow

to city wall, to portal, we enter
the night city's narrow passages,
men and women there sit
on silent stone, faces

buried in hands, silent
or weakly shaking, eyes closed,
so much the incarnation of moaning
petals, no one sees

us across the night to the point
where Gato fades beside
the distant portal and disappears
amid the night soul.

CAUSEWAY

The far portal points from the city
away and out to the night
sky, dark trees and island end
there at black waters edge,

there one figure in absent light,
lone woman in black huipil,
her long hair darkest burgundy
integral to this night of hours,

she motions me come to her,
I try to speak but she fills
the air with words in tones
sure as they are sad: I will take you

to Mictlan, we will cross the sad
night waters across to reach
the distant shore, the white place,
Mictlan, a place of souls at rest, place

of blank peace, and place you seek,
meaningful place. She is Xeritzin,
mother of sterile and fertile birth,
she speaks the dead's language, takes

my hand and leads to island
terminus to the path that parts
black waves and points to
white land, the northern land.

The causeway fades off far
ahead into blind night
the only sounds, our feet, the waves,
her bare feet kick up bits of bone

that the spine of dirt holds,
she runs to long wave sounds,
to sorrows unlike petals but greater
perdition, till we reach path's end,

gray flags mark the final exit,
a pale dog waits for us
at causeway end and gray
land extends beyond.

Xeritzin motions me still,
removes black huipil and gently covers
the pale dog's head, she motions
that I follow her past,

off the sorrowful path and forward.
In the graying light I see
her back, skin covered in
cipher of cihuatl, an image

of childbirth I make out
as light transforms a lighter gray,
and then in the distance, white

13 *White*

MICTLAN

Light envelopes Xeritzin, me,
earth tones transform lighter
ahead our every step,
all there reflects all there,

all the long and short of wave
earth glow before us,
sky is fog, fog billows here,
there, and clean brilliant

light in holes between,
for it is a northern land
place of undifferentiated spectrum,
place of bright peace.

My guide points out the souls
at rest who neither see us nor care
as we walk among them, some
reveal faces as if in dream,

others stare at blank codices
as if only to comprehend.
She speaks to one, to others,
their blank eyes blank,

in a language I have never heard,
yet as we walk further white,
the words become intelligible,
bit by bit I learn the concerns

of a young man, and blush in shame
at the words of an old woman.
We press on, the ground becomes sand
like sand in Tulum, and the air,

transparent except where white.
More steps, more souls and we come
to the tlamatini, and beyond, the poet.

ARISTOTLE

The first point, ¿is it? regards
the matter of the real, for what
am I here, but image of my other
self, in this final place, Mictlan,

yes, where all are hard image
against a pervading white
except for questioning poets,
like yourself, and their guides, Xeritzin

here, Virgil, yet if the primary
regards the real, is the first look
a look upon illusory reality
as your paper songs say, mere

shadows cast by infernal glare?
Yes, and further, the site of such
real comes to mean only by
the arc of poets, your acts,

here in this place, Mictlan means true
reflection fashioned in your words,
by the flowers you sing of dead past,
yes, but how can the first point

be fashioned of itself indivisible,
being just self and nothing more,
singularly, but point one? an identity
of self reflection, point one before

the first number, the double, and before one
there can be nothing absent, each point,
part of line, bit of cube, is whole,
yes, a hole, and so a full zero

completes itself, no, no thing
absent, so the image shadow
soul motioning in a white field,
point one, is the identity of self

which cannot be hole because otherwise
impossible? each soul is hole, yet
only known by living poesis or the gods,
but here, is mere white reflection

of that, and yet truly, Equis,
tlahcuiloco of floricanto, as well
as Gato and Xeritzin and all other
souls alive, live only in the inks,

in the red and the black, for only in
codices do bodies truly animate,
do you imagine the incidents of death,
your father, my teacher's teacher,

are held only there? are a line
of events only in relation,
only incidents of history?
know this, you come to life

in the cantos I sing, your acts
your body, so many petals lying
on white sand, gain color
but not fact, in the poems, your line,

its cross, and the points it divides
are simple fact and not true,
for it is the flower and the song
that marks the sole zero,

that marks difference, not one.

MARIE UGUAY

Xeritzin takes me from the Tlamatini
leads to where white sand
stops cold, to where white heaps
snow cold below dunes

of cold fog spill one last exit,
to where there in the snow,
the face of a woman lies
perfect face, this poet,

dark hair, pale lips and a white skin
lost in snow. Xeritzin
kneels and lets red hair drape
over the cold face and across,

presses her lips to hers,
the eyes open, the face
speaks to my guide of me,
son corps est un point fixe,

but here in Mictlan, life beyond,
she gathers petals from three rivers
for song and sings to me
je vous porte dans vos silences historiques,

beyond the whole wave the dead
and real, bercé revêtue
par la blancheur infernale du jour,
the frozen coordinates of flame

and the true, and yet I pause
before the perfect face
and ask if she is probable,
not fact, but true, and if her breath

is bright fog or verbal reflection
of codex ink, and Xeritzin's
body marks, a floricanto
of life beyond. She whispers

in my ear, Xeritzin exhales
fog and steps back, back
in the brilliant white, and I
cup snow in my own hands and cover

the perfect face.

3/3: CALIFORNIA NO ES ISLA

14 *Polylogue*

ONE SITE, TWO SOULS, HOUR ZERO

Peninsula-tepic
Lola Arc and other poet
l'outre-heure

◆

Hill at peninsula end point
inscribed by water, a vapor air,
she, cool northern light,
he follows fault lines where
time can only describe
hour dreams and impossible daze

◆

Pacific, gulf and bay
define la Isla California,
Cabos to Saint Francis,
where Lola moves in words and dance
mnemotechny, he draws ink
live action, prepares to imagine
lines of imaginary syntax without
ordinal syntactic corps, for no first word
is made from zero night mimesis

◆

The north peninsular extreme, so altern,
red bridge instead of rock arch,
the ocean ends inland and white
fog spills white all summer white,
Lola refuses change back to fleshless
philosopher's daughter, still she runs tidal sand,
and graciously he accepts water, the fluid held by hyper-
cooled fluid, he speaks and hears, and why not?
speech is enabled by shifting proximities even if empty
of any real river of hours, hearing, even if distance and spin
made sense without linear desire and transformation
meant locus and point and motion.

◆

This site, meters uphill, breathes hard,
vantage point at bay, 122 by 37, context of particular
earth and sky and sea and fog in motion
circumscribes her face and perfect word, she imagines
vanilla orchids, he, a hummingbird, perfectly
hover, still, unbelievably quick,
a flap in no time change merely beside the
smaller distance of flower and changes all at altern
angles, altern light from holes in opaque night

◆

City of streets, landfill full of abandoned ships,
singular arc of one sole sun
illuminate ciphers she shapes by moving hand
as well as the font he imagines full
not at the moment, instance without instants,
full motion across dead time, pale of history

◆

Peninsular cityscape points in sky
where she lives, he reflects
lost continuity, contiguous typeface

15 *Ordinal Syntax*

This angle of sun, phase of moon,
gluon proximate quark
can never will be
can never were,
but for a taut tense schema,
grapheme and phoneme,
red and at times harmonious,
that relates artist line to human form,
lyric, to mito doloroso
its grammar but orders beyond life
never life.

Imagine a man with fingertip stained ink
draws the Virgen de Guadalupe
he wants sacred, her face is perfect, radiates,
but the stain nags, random,
intimate, blood red or blood black
not part of the arc drawing, perhaps
erase the mark under rapture
or conceive all reality lies in it only?
or peel back skin tomorrow or not take up pen
hours ago as the taut tense makes real?
One absent flower does not exist, nor
its virtual progeny, and here
this live conjunction is already dead.

16 *Vida Nueva*

Font is not
the perfect typeface
but metonym that holds
the perfect frøzen accident
that resounds and shines
any place I go

Some there she holds me
by the margins, gathers
petals and leaves
changes her red heart,
radiates yellow,
holds black thorns
against a white snow

act zero

Sin Control

See, if flesh, yes, were made fish
carnal made sea flesh, blood
and wine, water, like glasses full of lake,
panes with fishes,
a stream, a sea, made so, see,
if so, why speak, desire, make verse?
If we, yes, we were chairs of fish
or we, pains and fishes, translucent,
transubstantial sea, see? Net sea?

En lugar de la nada

Marta swims the shallows to my house,
cleaves the Heraclitus moss effortlessly
from the Spanish more than chiasmus
y les vagues du fascisme:
alma de agua de morte, mais más a o a solo
solids of water from moss plus two currents to psyche
Là en lugar de nadar, son corps nettoie l'eau
by vague outline heat lines
ripple the air, her strokes, a water.
Marta swims a solid purity shaped like spear
in Mediterraneans damned at Ceuta,
no other soul nada for nothing
for nadie rests chez nous.

Inspiración

En el film, es ella, la extranjera,
ella que conmueve al protagonista
fingido en la blancura de la luz
y en el negro del infinito también
simplemente a causa de hablar francés.
En la escena que recuerdo, ella para,
espera a las lluvias de guerra, bueno,
metáforas de conflicto y de sangre
pero lluvias todavía, tal como
lluvias son al momento de encontrarse
con un acto de belleza violenta:
el mármol de una mano de una diosa
se compromete bajo la redacción
como la memoria aún persistente.
Es, según el guión improvisado,
la belleza que demora y no la actriz,
es la raza de olas y la de mareas
que simplemente son sus familiares,
es el paisaje que es sexo para ella
más que la respiración de las lomas,
los sueños de los impasibles robles.
Pero en la tarde, afuera en la plaza,
ella está sola y fuera de la imagen,
fuera del montaje y de la historia
envuelta en una sintaxis helada
como si fueran piedras las palabras.
Con eso, la figura de la mujer
conoce ambos la escultura y las lluvias
pero algo de las palabras francesas
ella no sabe nada:
porque reproducida el habla falla
y la respiración da vida a nadie.
Al reconocer el nombre de la actriz
y de la figura que ella simula,
Veronica Karina,

ves por fin las letras F-I-N
que ilusionan el impulso del guión,
allí, lejos en la larga distancia
donde negra está la pantalla gris
y cierras a la vez la última blanca
página del libro, F-I-N.
¿Apagar la luz en ese momento
o esperar un poquito?
Cierras los ojos tal como el libro
y después de haber librado la vista
de todos los trozos blancos y negros
de pantalla y página, luz y papel,
mueves la cabeza a la derecha y ves
el azul cielo desde el avion azul
desde las alturas por la ventana
ves la azulada sangre que flota
encima lo de abajo, casa y plaza,
encima memorias desvanecidas.
A la vez que ves, al mismo instante
dos mariposas llegan a tu cama
por fin llegan a las manos que apenas
dejan caer un libro desde el cielo.
Respiras sobre las frágiles alas,
a la cama te caes y se te ocurre
que los sueños no han sido los efectos
de muerte ni las causas de belleza.
Traes en la mano, musa,
las alas azules de haber vivido
bajo un cielo que no está hecho de imagen
cuando respiras tu respiro encima.

Illumination Mine

it is after all
this faith blind in light
after everything enlightening
more is the brighter god

omni omni omni

by design illumines all
small bones conceal little
between ultraviolet
and infrared
the meek prey on the spit
of sand bare between
the blue-violets
of sea, sky, and sea

the divine color
a bleach of revelation
more and more light
and faith in the more

the word god shines
there for the taking
burns away any
possible night
all seeing
seizing all

Four Portraits in Water

I. THE STORY OF WATER

The music of water comes in some part from its aspect not motion and not in beat of seas on shore, but from the element visual, from the tiny arc of light the little degree of the 360 that emanates from our solar star, the tiny degree that enters our black pupil and makes the entire world of all we see: and in this fact she finds the knowing of sea set loose in sight, without the shadow of constraint and masculine awe, and thus viewing she is set free. It is a music, like music, the spirit of music, in how it collects heat and takes shape, a cup of hand, a palm of bay, a holding of its liquidity, translucent and wet. In the beginning she puts one finger in water, puts it to her mouth tastes the cycle that constructs life and herself rains like desert rain, like lake effect rain, like a tropic that she is actually: tears are human rain, she is translucent and wet, she is tiny arc of all that can be seen and that beyond sight: it is a cycle confirmed in the music of water. Drop, splash, wave, a thick liquid the density of life and with salt, some sort of release, perhaps a diminished chord, perhaps a beat of part one, perhaps the taste of wine.

to envision read imagine to read and sing

The succession of event, its incidence, is wave. succession from sweat to drop of rain.

The lyric, she points out, if aqueous, must be saline, sea rather than river, gulf rather than stream, and if coeval, then vital at the waters' crash in surf. Her point, simple, if aqueous, then I must be saline, by force, and if coeval, then vital, oceanic

She imagines my body aqueous saline. if aqueous then saline, if alive, then ocean. vital oceanic It is significant that river meets sea in a clash of salinity, for two species split at liquid light and liquid sound, waves the color of and waves of the sound surf What do we make of the white light of the surf break and the white noise too?

Chrome Yellow, Smooth, Echo

come home, a cross
of prime light as god's breath
across once gentle fields as
warm psyche in spires
calls for faith
beside faces one fact

Forget the course again, that time spent in part had been one separation
or that the recollection of agony could detail so long, the long path if so shone:
each sole inch of darkness, after all, could have held whatever imagined: one
cold heart of iron pounded to steel, hurled in sharp points: a cloth of so many
tears revealing a cross section of sponge, yet flesh, yet blood. For that war is scar
only. That smoke more dust on dirt only. It has been settled. The heart cannot
be rebroken.

The moment light
releases new chrome
yellow from sun
the tiny arcs make
warm the eye new
beside the once lost
and without meaning
minutes ago

The tiny few rays,
arc to you because
of gravity, of course,
that weighs you down
you light as an object
without wait you
alight in a metaphor of fire
that reveals
and obliterates at once
the long history called night:
one burning spire,

one site of one flesh
proximate burns
rapid, coeval,
oxidation in sight

What else but that bright element of home yellow consists like unbroken surface, like so much that was not, not the jagged night, its rupture nor spill? Unimpeded chrome as if a gain the issue in spires were noon and first illumination at once one. O bright home this course, again a gain of course.

APPENDIX 1

Previously Uncollected Poems

Two poems from the draft manuscript of *Act Zero* not included in the published book

Balance

La carte de l'équilibre, map de escribir,
qui occupe tu ser is the plane
space de l'arbre dans la veine
de ville, vida mía, ainsi where
you take city matte bits,
piedritas déplacées, pressées
to your lips asina como
entiendo yo, así. C'est une carte
de défit, a feat féroce frente
a la naturaleza del fuego. C'est une peau
formée par cône qui organise
the night sky performed. C'est l'objet
constitué du souffle, muralla de espiritus,
city wall of psyche, estrellada y
enviada para effacer les contes de la douleur
sad and bright et confusée. On one side,
un positionnement numérique
se extiende como si a través de la vida,
on the other, un ordre est poussé
jusqu'aux étoiles. Sin habler dime
que ce n'est pas aussi. My mongrel
joy before such story existe
comme si fait étranger, comme
si fragment fortuit, as if
la verdad before certain stream.

Xochitepec

Words of another.
Otro Autor

Within this construct there portends
le travail de l'architecte étranger,
"xochitepec" is after all
flor y montaña, fleur et montagne,
the site de la femme, philologically
fille de logique, flower of the mountain,
floral display in xochitl in cuicatl
or hill of song, cuicatepec, ainsi.

Or, again, why should atl signify
water, ¿agua en los dibujos
del arquitecto? et rien plus?
Place of water, lugar de nadar,
as if it meant what it means, mere
paseo florido, rumbo frío, laissé pour mort,
des mots malencontreusement simples
like earth and nature and height.

Celtic Fractal

She is the words
small pale woman,
not the faint trace
red touch I make.

She is the words
small pale woman,
not submaxillary ah
intermittent burst
machine like humming
bird in high weed
when seams align
allowing sound the
small and internal
electric motor
whirr.

She is the words
small pale woman,
not the morphemes
of sex
words.

Poem published only in Stanford Humanities Review *3.1 (1993), 22.*

APPENDIX 2

Collaborative Poem: Alfred Arteaga, Anna Kazumi Stahl, and David Lloyd

This previously unpublished poem a collaborative work produced in 1995 by Alfred Arteaga, Anna Kazumi Stahl, and David Lloyd. Modeled on the surrealist game "exquisite corpse," the poem was composed over e-mail according to a protocol whereby each writer in turn sent only the second of a pair of lines to the next writer in order, who then responded with two further lines, of which only the second was sent on to the next writer in the sequence. The whole poem was assembled at the end of a given number of exchanges, before which no individual participant had seen the work as a whole.

Tres Tigres Tristes

This is how it begins, an unfolding of things.
Were I to ask for something more by so simple an act
As the rain at work across the trellis

the percolation of sighs in the weather
whether real it be or not, oh fine,
but why such a bitter mind, he asked, touched the

pentameter of the machine, the iamb of tooled alloy
angry (for the metallic scan of metallic touch
those barriers, the who's your neighbor bray,

the whole knowable community's in bits
and I am too, I've half a mind to go and half to stay
the four winds never cross or meet in my day, why

four? Wherefore wind, times four, winds plural
one, the motion of atoms, two, the birth of wind, twice
the burden recurs

at all, at all
at all or none the lottery will run and the lucky will
be an instant entry visa holder welcome black to scum liberty

welcome to free. But why such bitter freedom, given the choices
we face. An entrance, a face, a confrontation of here, now
from these overhearings projects you, unbound

to the ends of the corrugated strip, flecks of fear tracking
the rippled steel, and in the ruts, the spill of
tears, the quick rip hidden, she watches him to see if he will

steal her tears, ignore the rift like water. So what is her
sense of this? What is his? An answer is so easy to construct
off of the long song of the strings, D minor

layer upon layer laid down without ending in view
las capas de las multitudes
y en ellas se da la altitud, la brevedad, the endless view

de lo que consisten las alturas, los altos sin fin
of the finite view, night vista, light view, of endless scope.
The third movement begins. We reach back

along the hot tracks for the shortest circuit around
the circuit breaks and the temperature leaps the streets
by the wrong side, someone shouts Hey! hot

cool like, by the wrong lake, just to the foreign side.
Me pagan in English and Spanish at the same time, hey
pero el precio del sudor nunca se paga, si viene

el viento del pueblo, viene con el olor de naranjas y de la piel de los ninos
naranjo en flor, somebody is singing oh the voice is a wind no one hears, but
everybody is brushed and met, naranjo en flor, the far in us all

the way gone. Every body in flight as if the grove were the
field below, the grove itself the site of flora so
pained with the waste, bent backs

and knuckles grazing the poison soil
brazen under the heels, mirthful still
mirthful resolute

resolving revolution. Que hay que hacer? Asi estamos
mesclados, revueltos, hambrientos, en busca de algo
you might have thought the corpse, filled with vague breath

was alive and multiplying
paranoia on the prairie
the mirth and the hazard of the many

virgens martyred in a catholic way. In a way,
a religious persistence, a symbol of stigmata
stymies me here, the invocation

of monsters looming from the chiaroscuro
obscure oscuro loom me leave me
free chiaro I am monster with thee but without I

am and am in truth: for this is the sole reason
I can stand here this way knowing I mean
and mean intensely: figuras, figuras, figures

in their eyes, figures in their faces
and voices, the press of absent hands a presence
words my mother's mother knew but I'm the first to say

so to end. It is the final of final instance,
the last one end. The first to say so ends the
ravelled threads, cut off at the pass, streaming at

the border, at the selvedge, at
the very edges of the precious faces, the final
breaths, sweet mezcla, musgo, un brote, at the end, fuiste, voz.

APPENDIX 3

The Original Texts of Cartas: *Alfred Arteaga and Carolina González*

These letter poems were exchanged between Alfred Arteaga and Carolina González in 1993–1994, and Arteaga's poems were included as a sequence in the volume *Red* with mostly minor revisions, sometimes—but not always—to standardize an occasionally idiosyncratic usage of Spanish and without the address line that originally concluded each one. They are included here, with thanks to Carolina, as a register of Arteaga's dialogical impulse and to furnish the initial context of the poems to which they were responding.

Carolina González is a former academic and journalist, careers that intertwined in her time studying Comparative Literature at the University of California, Berkeley. Originally from New York and Santo Domingo, Dominican Republic, she now lives in Brooklyn, New York, and works for the labor union 32BJ SEIU, which represents building service workers.

19.2.1993

1 *Escrito en agua*

AA

Se acaban los seis años de sequía
fácilmente: dedos de agua llegan
por fin a la cara seca, la cara retirada.
La casa, la camisa,
traspasada por lluvia demasiado
atenta, se convierten en líneas
de versos de bestias de selvas de hojas de papel
secas, mojadas, remojadas.
Por seis años una California sin
canto, sin ganas existía. El color de aire,
agua es algo común. Se dicen
que no existe en el desierto,
pero fíjate: hay bastante en sombra y letra
para creer en vida por toda la vida y además
para terminar una época seca, para matar
silencio en las hojas.

Berkeley, California

2 MARZO 1993

2 *Tormenta tropical*

CG

Ese fué uno de los hallazgos
del recuerdo:
envuelto en un instante
fluido y apretado como un puño de seda,
el aire se anuda en el pulmón,
en la piel áspera de cemento tiznado
una angustia óptica arropa todo
y con una cuerda de guitarra tensada hasta casi llorar
las nubes rompen fuente.
Arroyos espontáneos corren calle abajo
alborotados como niños en recreo
arrastrando flotillas de flores y basura.
Qué curioso, el Caribe se sosiega,
arrullado por una caricia de agua
que sólo el agua comprende a plenitud.
Entretanto, la tierra se encarama por mis pies descalzos,
hasta llenarme la nariz,
mejor que una cruz cenicienta para recordar
que no es polvo estéril lo que seremos
sino lodo que vuelve a la vida
como los helechos incansables que se
adueñan de toda pared.
Y así de fácil retiran su súbito beso
dejando luz lavada y escurrida,
la piel citadina aliviada de su fiebre,
y palabras acuosas entre estos dedos arrugados.

Santo Domingo, Caribe

12.3.93

3 *Trozos*

AA

Si pedazo no tiene una esencia propia
y a la vez, es la pura verdad que
nunca alcanzaremos un cuerpo móvil
que ya ha arrancado ayer,
¿cómo podemos comunicar? A pedazos
llegaremos, tantas aguas diáfanas, cuando
la luz reteblanca se quiebra encima
la mesa y revela si mismo
esencialmente: lo que es una gota a otra, es
tal trozo humano a tal fragmento
nocturnal de la ciudad, es isla
a la marea menguante:
pasos claros, ocultos, atraviesan el mar
lago, laguna, lágrima, huellas
en las pieles de una agua quebradiza,
fronteriza, traspasada no más con un cambio
de ser, una pausa al medio corriente,
hasta bruma, vapor, o humedad necia.
Claro, se trasluce y se vierte en seguida,
el blanco pedazo del sagrado blanco,
y sin esencia, enajenan todos los
fragmentos, insensibles.
¿Qué hay? ¿Qué cae?

Berkeley, California

4 *Ciudad amor*

CG

Volver a esta tierra salada
como a un amante
íntimamente desconocido
no sé por qué
los sueños los recuerdos y
una imaginación voluntariosa se
confunden tercamente
y las caricias vacilan
casi extraviadas
porque esta rodilla
ese árbol
no debería tornearse así.
Qué calle qué grito qué hueco
en qué brazos
me encuentro porque hay
otras ciudades otros amores hasta
otros mares rumbeando este cuerpo
y si Blondie en Gazcue
o un nopal en la Sarasota
turban el acuerdo espacio-tiempo
perdóname
ese glíglico ajeno no lo provoca
la nostalgia
(que también se llama miedo a la traición)
sino una lógica nómada
(es decir, afincarse en el tambaleo)
que, sonámbula, trueca los hábitos
y es el cariño, digo, que desgaja
las vivencias y las hace
pedazos de papel.

1.4.93

5 *Varias respuestas*

AA

La música, por ejemplo,
existe al momento.
Su recuerdo nos engaña
precisamente porque es
mentira. El dibujo que miras
después de cerrar los ojos
no se distingue mucho
de cualquier foto o pintura: es
algo visto, es algún ser. Lo que
puedes detener, parar en media
vuelta, es algo, claro, pero no es
vuelta, ni corriente, ni ritmo.
La vida, por ejemplo, cruza
líneas y nos desengaña
aunque creemos el contrario:
no es cosa, ni tiene ser.
Los versos se despiden así,
acuérdate. Los huesos se despiden
así. Tantos ecos, así.

Berkeley, California

14 ABRIL 93

6 *La clave*

CG

Onda, ola.
Una, tropieza y gira
en su severa profundidad,
la otra se desliza mansa en un saludo marino,
pero ambas cintas sonoras, hermanas en fin.
Basta de física.
No explica ni instruye
sólo deshace el diseño tejido
hebra a hebra, nota a nota.
El destiempo al oído
que, desesperado, se disminuye,
pretende ordenar,
buscar el punto entrópico,
no decir "caos"
ante el sancocho sónico barrial.
Si en una bachata percibo
un eco mamey de calipso
la tergiversada guitarra africana
notas saltamontes, pausas abruptas,
¿la hace menos situada?
Si motor y botella
pueden ser pieles de tambor
si sabor corresponde a ahuyentar la muerte espiritual
y es el sonido, más que palabras
que nos permite mentarnos mutuamente,
la mentira es el verso quedo
la inmobilidad del cuerpo escribiente.

Santo Domingo, Caribe

24.4.93

7 *La joda española*

AA

Si por muerte entendemos el sereno
y por vida entendemos lo sereno . . .
No.
Si está lleno el autobús de desconocidos
hasta dormidos unos
pero sé bien de dónde vengo y más o menos
a qué hora acabaré . . .
Mejor.
Cuando te veo de paso me pongo a dormir,
si por paso entendemos el tráfico ilegal
y por "tú" y "yo" entendimos la misma cosa . . .
Sí.
Largos están los caminos reales hasta la muerte
y qué pena dar una mala vuelta: a los lados, afilado,
no es hielo, es vidrio, es espejo, es nada.

Berkeley, California

6 MAYO 1993

8 *Ruta cotidiana*

CG

Cada semáforo puede ser
cruce potente entre vida y muerte
deidad y humano.
Recuerdo autobuses inmaculados
en camino al olvido mismo
donde sólo van ancianos y pobres
con orgullo tan reducido que
sobraba espacio para dos.
Pero guagua no es autobús
como beso no es en inglés,
me lo dice la dulce paciencia
en la cara sobre kakis sudando charol
la gracia de la mujer falda estrecha
se coloca sin derramar
una sola gota de muslo.
El cobrador tiene alas de rayón
pies amagando aterrizaje cada instante.
Me miran extraña.
¿Maldigo mi piel por no ser terruño?
Como raíces igual
tengo lengua que no vale tragar,
desdoblada encrucijada,
suficiente para el camino,
y aunque te cuento con palabras,
quizás basta, quizás es algo.

Santo Domingo, Caribe

29.5.93

9 *Palabras masculinas*

AA

Mentira pura la letra,
la desesperanza, la fortaleza:
mentira pura el dios inhábil
de las tres cruces, tres veces
desocupado: mentira las nubes
que mienten y que se hacen
tales ficciones: y más mentira
fiel amor que arde hasta el hueso,
irradiando lo que no puede quemar.
Pura mentira pura la pureza de la
mentira más mentida. No es que no más
no creo en las letras: no
creo que existen: aquí sólo yo grito
solamente en la plena luna,
"mentira." Por eso vale el sexo:
sí puede mentir pero, ¿para qué?
Si es o no es, no me importa,
lo que vale no cuenta.

Berkeley, California

12-21 JUNE, 1993

10 *Partir*

CG

Duele en los huesos
dislocados por el arranque
en la sangre que se licúa
bajo la levedad de los cielos.
Granos de sal que rehusan derretirse
que en vez brotan verdes
tiñen las aguas, manchan mis ojos.
Ahora comprendo el dolor de las raíces
la tristeza de las hojas
que las semillas lloran la necesidad de su vagar.
Malditas horas que se burlan
una tras otra tras otra
tierra y mar que se ensanchan
recordándote débil y desnuda y atada.
Y la única contraburla posible
como siempre el sexo:
el mismo cuerpo que limita
por un ahora un aquí
reúne todos los mares en nuestras oleadas
todas las playas las tierras cambiantes
los días oscuros las temporadas perdidas
en un piadoso beso de disolución.
Morder lo púrpura del horizonte
desplazar la nostalgia intraducible
aunque no aguante
y las promesas queden igual de flojas
y aún los deseos se descoloren
me lanza
me lanzo.

Caribe–NY–SF

19/9/93

11 *Aparte ir*

AA

Después de la muerte del tono,
queja de la línea telefónica,
persiste el recado, son y paso
de la estructura del danzón: estampías
desplegadas con cartas blancas: qué
selvas matinales, maritales, qué danza
marginal, qué pelo negro. Así
desenmarañan nuestras piernas así,
tuya, mía, mía, tuya:
la trensa que un día nos hicimos
desenreda, y el doble hélice
que enlaza a tí y él que enlaza a mí,
día con día, también: tal como
pierna y pelo, el ADN. Aparte
te vas, me voy: la distancia
en los matorrales.

Berkeley, California

25 SEPTIEMBRE 93

12 *Mente sola*

CG

Demasiadas noches
los miembros fantasmas
cuando se aleja
el viejo temor
de no abrazar el temblor
que cierne la vida de vez en cuando
y queda espacio para
espasmos de
de la porosidad de la piel
de los hábitos de dos.
Antes bailaba el cambio
otro danzante, otro paso
y todavía desconfío de
la unión de buzones, de hambres,
de pelo (largos los dos,
el cuero casi todo velludo)
Más palabras hacen falta,
sin embargo por momentos
las aborrezco aquí, sólo quiero
húmedo y caliente
café, ducha, sábana.

La misión, San Francisco

10.11.93

13 *Rama*

AA

No hay versos en los árboles,
pero sí hay papeles.
No hay aduanas en los romances,
pero hay pistolas.
No hay nada que tomar en el hospital,
no más hay tiempo.
No hay bastantes horas,
sólo rinde el cambio.
No hay nada más que tristes monedas en la iglesia,
más el crucifijo.
No se halla cura en un perdido veneno,
porque las aguas de reflexión ocupan espacio:

Cae la catedral y sube el agua a la vez
a causa del reflejo y el ser de la superficie del lago,
y refluyen más allá de los orígines ocultos,
olvidados, o perdidos.

Berkeley, California

20 FEBRERO 1994

14 *Domingo de palma*

CG

El momento ya se escurre, sin embargo:
aparte de la memoria, sé qué
me detiene frente a la palma
sol de frente, nubarrón frío detrás.

en este papel, la frase
"en el exilio
la única casa es la escritura"
me hace reír
esto no es exilio, pero sería pendeja
una casa de letras o cartas.
espero no creas es sólo casa que busco
en ceniza, en lengua de leche,
algún consuelo,
en el vocabulario de la lluvia.

Mi sangre, no más paradójica que la de Cristo,
se repone sólo para brotar, ya haga o no
comparación a cualquier sufriente.
Presumo y me planto, porque es el estribillo
que reconozco este esto ni es exilio
y comoquiera para contrarrestar los sueños.

¿Te das por vencido? La adivinanza
te la cuento mañana. Presumo y me planto; que mejor decir
la tentación a la mudez. No es cuestión de buscar mejor sitio en la mesa
ni lugar seguro en la acera
sino poder decir mi propio camino.

La misión, San Francisco

18.4.94

15 *Coordinada*

AA

Después del abandono, traición,
desprecio, rechazo, huida, aburrido,
amor obsesionante, amor pura, mera y honra,
muerte del hijo, primer beso, carta tarde,
y el perder de todo menos ella,
permanece lo más pobre que nos da la ciencia.
Las coordinadas Cartesanas localizan
cualquier cuerpo humano en el espacio:
equis, i griega, y a veces, la zeta,
explican todo y nos ofrecen un consuelo
racional, que quiere decir, desapasionado.
Pero como llegamos a experimentar:
el cambio cambia a uno y a los dos,
el sujeto no es igual a, ni se refiere
a, su pobre mismo. Nunca en ninguna vida.
El cuerpo tal como el alma no es número,
ni es el rumbo de la vida una ecuación linear.
Sólo dejamos con la probabilidad
y la estadística: ella esta aquí casi, quizás,
ahorita, parece. Y la coordinada nada vale.

Los Angeles

30 ABRIL 1994

16 *Resurreción*

CG

Me acusa a diario la física:
dos puntos en mismo espacio/tiempo
no van.
¿Y qué de trayectoria, de
múltiples factores sobre A y B
que dificultan curvas paralelas?
Y de lo pequeño que resulta un plano
de sólo dos ejes (aún de tres)?
Del cruce catastrófico
de regularidad maldita
con aquel punto perdido
con el tangente tan deseado.

El Caos ya es ciencia medible, dicen
y lo creo.
Sino cómo explicar que
el latido de mi corazón lleva un gemido,
moléculas que se abrazan y se empujan
a otra ciudad, aun bajo el agua
a otra isla con la marea
y el dolor, aunque siempre único,
es repetible.

No es cuestión de formular, de abstraer
de pelar la pasión con bisturí.
Dijo la de Asbaje que si Aristóteles
hubiese cocinado, cuán mejor su ciencia.
Y mi mente y mi corazón
no comen del mismo plato, pero comen
y la química es sólo los amoríos y las peleas
que tienen los elementos entre sí.

9.5.94

17 *Cuentos impasibles*

AA

1 luna para ti.
2 soles para que te ardes para mi.
3 dedos desmochados para ti.
4 papeles blancos para mi.
5 iglesias de carton.
6, para mi, vasos vacios de verdad.
7 cosas perdidas, como la sombra anoche.
8 veces solo.
9 corazones de piedras verdes para ti.
10 veces tarde para mi.
11 es nada y tu lo guardas bien.
2 soles para que te ardes para mi.

Los Angeles, Califas

23 MAYO 1994

18 *Malos pasos*

CG

Flojo ánimo, suelto verso
puta si mujer
perdida la razón
o las llaves, si quieres
o, para volver acá
el sol que entra sin invitación
y calcina mi último sueño
la luna que acaricia
Tras llevar, las palmeras
y los borrachos igual
la lámpara que acompaña
más fiel que soledad.

¿A dónde lleva la lengua
si no se frena la inteligencia?
¿Qué resta que sujeta
si el sentido no aguanta?

San Francisco, Califas

6.8.94

19 *La red*

AA

Una matriz es el abecedario,
o por lo menos, una serie estrellada,
una actriz desafortunada, acostumbrada
a dormir sola. Me desmiente en
media locución con su mudo perder:
cae abrazo a un acto desanimado, a pedazos,
lo que fuera el acto del brazo
cae a una significación, una avaricia
del deseo sin conexión al querer.
La telenovela conecta las quejas
de Hollywood o Churrubusco
a mi genio raso, estrellado ya.
Y la ausencia del caso no es una treta
temporal, pero acaso la red se anima
el fin de los angeles. Y en fin me quedo
preguntando, ¿porqué es feminina
la mano y masculino el ser? ¿Porqué
no entiendo nada de lo que he escrito?
¿Y porqué tropiezo tanto yo
sin sueño sin la red?

Los Angeles, Califas

23 JUNIO 1994

20 *El nudo*

CG

Aquí al fin del mundo
mil años no son nada
pero cuarenta sí insólitos
y cinco veranos ni se diga
Necedad si aguanta el amarre
a tal umbral o curva de gesto tierno.
Intruso este corazón
que rehusa
dividir sangre
que bulle deseante
de la que por ombligo cruza.
La cizaña debe arrancarse
¿pero por cuál raíz?
Enramada la conciliación
con el guión familiar
Nudo reanudo que
es ya más tela que hilo
más trenza que yagua.
Aquí no hay palabra
más que balbuceo
y lúnatica soy
sólo por temporada.

Nueva York

13.7.94

21 *Contrabando y natación*

AA

Pero, al acabar de desear,
¿cuáles aguas imaginadas?
Labios son libros en algún sentido.
Como impregnan las hojas y
se derraman las letras hasta
significación, y eso aunque
localizan lejos del borde de
los lagos del significado.
La mano sentida, dormida
la izquierda, frías las dos,
tratan de nadar como árboles
californios, como las manzanitas,
por ejemplo, en medio de una
niebla de comprender. Sí,
sí hay el trabajo de la boca, sí,
la pureza del tráfico nos emociona, y sí,
la encrucijada también.

Berkeley, Califas

13 SEPTIEMBRE 1994

22 *Desplazo barrial*

CG

Qué rebuscado el proceso:
resulta ser
el apareamiento
el motor de mis vagancias.
Pocas quedan las calles y consabidas
las horas de ambular,
aborrecidas las caras y siluetas
que ya ni reconozco ni persigo;
rehuyo mundos hechos
con fantasías ajenas
los cuartos oscuros
el humo dulzón
el descontrol de la caza.
¿De dónde la certitud de andar
trazo tan calcado?
¿Qué del espeluznante encanto
de cacofonía urbana, de
las faltas al sintaxis de cartas de loco amor?
Pasadas, encerradas, enterradas, suprimidas
aterradoras
por las llaves del deber.

San Pancho, Califas

NOTES

The poems collected in this volume were originally published by Alfred Arteaga in the book-length collections listed in the Select Bibliography (see pages 265–66). The editor of the present volume has regarded the texts of poems published in those books as the intended final versions of the poems, some of which were published previously in different form in magazines and other venues. To resolve editorial questions while preparing the text of this book, the editor also consulted original manuscripts, which helped clarify the poet's choices and intentions.

NOTES FOR THE POEMS

Notes for *Cantos*

Most of these notes were included by the author in the original book publication of *Cantos* and have been supplemented here by the editor of the present volume, as indicated in bracketed additions to the original notes.

The Cantos are not spoken in silence, and some, especially los primeros, respond to echoes and recall voice in time with voice.

["X antecanto," line 6: August 29, 1970, was the date of the massive Chicano Moratorium march in East Los Angeles. See Introduction, p. xvii.]

"Primero: Arrival," lines 8, 10, 12: Tupac Amarú, epigraph to part 3, "Los conquistadores," of Pablo Neruda's *Canto general*. [The lines cited by Arteaga are a variant of the last words in Quechua attributed to the Inca king and warrior Tupac Amarú, slightly misquoted by Neruda from a secondary source, "Ccollanan Pachacámac, Ricuy: Auccacunas Yahuarniy Richascancuta." ("Pacha Kamaq, witness how my enemies shed my blood."). See Pablo Neruda, *Canto general*, ed. Enrico Mario Santi (Madrid: Ediciones Cátedra, 1990), 143.]

"Primero: Arrival," lines 35–38: John Donne, Elegie XIX, "To His Mistris Going to Bed." [For the lines alluded to here, see Helen Gardner, ed. *The Metaphysical Poets* (Harmondsworth: Penguin Books, 1972), 54.]

["Primero: Arrival," line 56: the name Cuauhtémoc (the last Aztec Emperor) means "one who has descended like an eagle." See the allusions to eagles in the following lines.]

"Primero: Arrival," lines 70–74, 77–78: James Joyce, "Penelope," *Ulysses*. [Xochitepec: "hill of flowers," name of a city in Morelos, Mexico. Malintzin: Aztec name of Hernán Cortés's translator and mistress, in Spanish "Marina," known disparagingly in Mexican and Xicanx tradition as "La Malinche." For the source of the quotation "yes I said yes I will Yes," see James Joyce, *Ulysses*, ed. Hans Walter Gabler (New York: Random House, 1986), 643–44. The words cited are the final words of Molly Bloom's soliloquy that closes the novel.]

"Primero: Arrival," line 81: Gaspar Pérez de Villagrá, "Primer Canto," *La Historia de la Nueva México*. [The line "ella que en buen ora nasco" does not appear to come from Pérez de Villagrá's poem (see note to "Segundo: Textos vivos," lines 73–77), but to riff on a phrase that recurs throughout the medieval Spanish *Poema de Mio Cid*, "el que en buen ora nasco." See, for example, Cantar Primero, stanzas 49 and 52, in Anónimo, *Poema de Mio Cid*, ed. Pedro M. Cátedra (Barcelona: Editorial Planeta, 1985), 54–55.]

"Primero: Arrival," lines 88–94: Sor Juana Inés de la Cruz, "Asunción," 1676 and "San Pedro Nolasco," 1677. [See Sor Juana Inés de la Cruz, *Obras Completas: Volumen II, Villancios y Letras Sacras*, ed. Alfonso Méndez Plancarte (Toluca: Instituto Mexiquense de Cultura, 1994), 17 and 41–42. The first four lines cited in Nahuatl here are from the Tocotín that concludes "Asunción." The editor gives the following "literal translation" in Spanish by Ángel Maria Garibay: "Si ya te vas, / nuestra amada Señora, / no, Madre Nuestra, / Tú de nosotros te olvides": "If you are going, our beloved Lady, do not, Our Mother, forget us." See *Villancios y Letras Sacras*, 365. The final two lines of the stanza are from the Tocotín that concludes "San Pedro Nolasco," 1677. The editor again gives Garibay's translation of these lines as "Puede que me olvida" and "mi amo lo sabe": "You may forget me" and "my soul knows it." See *Villancios y Letras Sacras*, 375. The line "Mati itlatol ihiyo" is not in this Tocotín, but appears to consist of three Nahuatl words, know, language and breath. For more on Sor Juana's multi- or inter-lingual "crossover poetics," see Alfred Arteaga, "Tricks of Gender Xing," in *Chicano Poetics: Heterotexts and Hybridities* (Cambridge: Cambridge University Press, 1997), 44–65.]

["Primero: Arrival," line 101: Coatepec-Cihuatepec-Cuicatepec: Nahuatl: "Hill of the Snakes" (from coatl, snake); "Hill of the Woman" (from cihuatl, woman); and "Hill of Song" (from cuicatl, song or poem).]

"Segundo: Textos vivos," line 28: Marie Uguay, *L'outre-vie* [(Montréal: Éditions du Noroît, 1979). Marie Uguay was a French-Canadian poet from Montreal who died of cancer in 1981 at the age of twenty-six. She appears also in Arteaga's book *Red*, in "Love in the Time of Aftershocks" VII, and in *Frøzen Accident*, in the final poem of the sequence "Nezahualcoyotl in Mictlan."]

["Segundo: Textos vivos," lines 70–71: Quoted text is from *Las Sergas de Esplandían*, Book V of the Spanish medieval romance *Amadís de Gaula*, from which the name California is derived. See Arteaga, "Tricks of Gender Xing," 44].

"Segundo: Textos vivos," lines 73–77: Gaspar Pérez de Villagrá, "Primer Canto," La Historia de la Nueva México. [Phrases in these lines are assembled from the "Canto Primero" of Gaspar Pérez de Villagrá, *La Historia de la Nueva México*, ed. Felipe

I. Echinique March (México, DF: Instituto Nacional de Antropologia e Historia, 1993), 125–27.]

["Segundo: Textos vivos," line 80: The word "tezcatl" means mirror.]

["Segundo: Textos vivos," line 81: The meaning of the word "nechichauallano" remains obscure.]

["Segundo: Textos vivos," lines 85–90: Indigenous words (and words from other sources) in this passage and their English equivalents: "tlilli": charcoal, soot; "quecholli": flamingo; "tlapalli": blood; "ixochiuh": her flower; "xronotopxopan": a macaronic mix of Russianized Greek (*xronotop*), from critic Mikhail Bakhtin's term "chronotope" and the Nahuatl "xopan," spring; "xiuhtlacuilolli": "year paintings" (chronicles); "amoxcali": library; "krugozory" (Russian), conceptual horizon or world-view, also a term derived from Bakhtin; "xicancuicatl": a coinage meaning Xicano (or Chicano) and song. See more commentary on this passage in the Introduction.]

["Tercero: El viaje," line 1: Mictlan: Nahuatl land of the dead; Xopan, Spring; Tenochtitlan, capital city and religious center of the Aztecs, destroyed by Hernán Cortés and now the site of Mexico City.]

"Tercero: El viaje," lines 3–5, 22–25: Arthur Rimbaud, "Le bateau ivre" [in *Poésies, Une saison en enfer, Illuminations*, ed. Louis Forestier (Paris: Gallimard, 1973), pp. 94–97. Lines 3–5 consist of a loose Spanish translation of the first quatrain of Rimbaud's poem, and lines 22–25 are a loose English translation of lines from its penultimate quatrain].

["Tercero: El viaje," line 9: The word "mixtitlan" means "in the clouds."]

["Tercero: El viaje," line 13: The word "tentli" means edge, brim, or lip (see the poem of this name in *House with the Blue Bed*, p. 110); "yollotl," heart; "yolotia," inspire.]

["Tercero: El viaje," line 17: Bavieca, Tizón, and Colada: the horse and two swords of Ruy Diaz of Bivar, or El Cid; see *Poema de Mio Cid*, ed. Cátedra (Editorial Planeta, 1985), 90 and 120. The terms in lines 18–21 refer to the *castas* or mixed-race categories in use in Spanish America.]

"Tercero: El viaje," line 27: [Juan-Diego Oxomoco: a compound of Juan Diego, the indigenous convert who had a vision of the Virgin at Guadalupe in 1531, and Oxomoco, Aztec goddess of night, astrology, and the calendar.]

"Tercero: El viaje," lines 31–32: Gaspar Pérez de Villagrá, "Primer Canto," *La Historia de la Nueva México* [the phrase "plus ultra" is from *Historia de la Nueva México*, 125].

"Tercero: El viaje," lines 47–48: Arthur Rimbaud. "Le bateau ivre." [See the second quatrain in the edition cited above: *Poésies, Une saison en enfer, Illuminations*, ed. Forestier (Gallimard, 1973).]

"Tercero: El viaje," lines 63–75: William Carlos Williams. "Sunday in the Park." [See Book 2 of *Paterson* (New York: New Directions, 1963), 47–48 and 51–52.]

"Tercero: El viaje," lines 88–97: *Stars and Stripes*, Mexico City, 1848. [This citation of the US Army newspaper alludes to the St. Patrick's Battalion, or San Patricios, formed by Irishman John Riley with mostly Irish soldiers who deserted the US Army to fight on the Mexican side in the Mexican-American War. After the Battle of Churabusco, thirty captured San Patricios were executed at the moment of the fall of the citadel of Chapultepec. Other soldiers were punished for desertion by branding and flogging. On the San Patricios, see Robert Ryal Miller, *Shamrock and Sword: The Saint Patrick's Battalion in the U.S.-Mexican War* (Norman: University of Oklahoma Press, 1989).]

"Tercero: El viaje," lines 103–109: Carlos Fuentes, *Todos los gatos son pardos*. [Arteaga's citation here refers to the introduction to Fuentes's play *Todos los gatos son pardos* (México, D.F.: Siglo Veintiuno Editores, 1971), 6.]

"Tercero: El viaje," lines 110–16: Arthur Rimbaud, "Le bateau ivre." [These lines are a loose variant of quatrain 15 of Rimbaud's poem; see *Poésies, Une saison en enfer, Illuminations*, ed. Forestier (Gallimard, 1973).]

["5: Romance Blanco": In the book *Red*, this poem and "6: Corrido Blanco" were on facing pages, since they're paired.]

"6: Corrido Blanco," lines 3–4: Sor Juana Inés de la Cruz. "Respuesta a Sor Filotea de la Cruz." [See Sor Juana Inés de la Cruz, *Obras Completas: Volumen IV: Comedias, Sainetes y Prosa*, ed. Alberto G. Salceda (Toluca: Instituto Mexiquense de Cultura,1994), 440–75. In "Respuesta," Sor Juana responded to a letter from a bishop who had censured her writing, citing the words of St Paul: *Mulieres in Ecclesia taceant*, "let women be silent in church (1 Corinthians 14:34)." For his commentary on this work of Sor Juana's, see Arteaga's essay "Tricks of Gender Xing" in *Chicano Poetics*, 1997.]

["muñeca, muñequita" and "world-echo, little world-echo": Again, in their original book layout these paired poems were on facing pages, which wasn't possible in this collection.]

"9: The Small Sea of Europe": Epigraph: Gayatri Chakravorty Spivak. [From Spivak's essay "Can the Subaltern Speak?" See *Marxism and the Interpretation of Culture*, eds. Cary Nelson and Lawrence Grossberg (Urbana: University of Illinois Press, 1988), 271–313.]

"10: À mon seul désir": Title, "À mon seul désir," from the tapestry, Musée de Cluny. [In this note, Arteaga refers to the sixth of a set of six tapestries depicting "The Lady and the Unicorn," the first five of which have titles that allude to each of the senses. The meaning of the title of this sixth tapestry, "À mon seul désir," remains obscure. See "17: fear" in *House with the Blue Bed* (pages 83–84 in this book) for more comments by Arteaga about this title phrase.]

"12: Letters of Color": Epigraphs: Juan Felipe Herrera, "Noche Verde Nuclear" [in Àkrilika (Santa Cruz, CA: Alcatraz Editions, 1989), 102–103]; Lorna Dee Cervantes, "Meeting Mescalito at Oak Hill Cemetery" [in *Emplumada* (Pittsburgh: University of Pittsburgh Press, 1981), 10]; Rosario Castellanos, "Poesía no eres tú." [from "En la tierra de en medio" in *Poesía no eres tú: Obra Poética 1948–1971* (México, D.F.: Fondo de Cultura Económica, 2004), 311. For comments that may shed light on "12: Letters of Color" and also "14: Respuesta a Frida," see "22: color" in *House with the Blue Bed*, on pages 97–99 in this book.]

"14: Respuesta a Frida": Epigraph: Marie Uguay, *L'outre-vie*, 9].

Notes for *House with the Blue Bed*

Since most of the historical and cultural references in this one of Arteaga's books are either explained in context or can be easily looked up, no explanatory notes seem necessary. Some biographical context to the work will be found in the Introduction (see xxv*ff*).

Notes for *Red*

Epigraph for the book: from the song "Amenece" (1988) by the Mexican rock band Caifanes.

"Diversos": The book *Red* (2000) opened with the first and last three poems of the earlier book *House with the Blue Bed* (1997), though in a different order: "Tentli," "Driving in Fog," "Blood, Sand, Blood," and "Amor y Caos" (to which was added the dateline "7/15/95 París"). Since these poems were otherwise unrevised, they appear here with the poems of *House with the Blue Bed* and have been omitted from the section "Diversos" in this book's presentation of *Red*.

"BC": The epigraph for this poem is from Christina Rossetti's poem "In an Artist's Studio," composed 1856 and published posthumously in 1896. In Rossetti's original, "dream" is singular. The personae of Arteaga's poem appear to be fictional.

"Tomorrow Today," "Lebensraum," and "Prayer for the Death of the Soul": For the political context of these poems see the Introduction to this book. *Das Gringo Volk braucht Lebensraum*: "The Gringo people needs space to live," alluding to the Nazi demand for "Lebensraum" that drove their expansion into Central Europe and the Soviet Union.

"Cartas": This sequence in *Red* consists of slightly revised versions of Arteaga's contributions to a poetic dialogue with Carolina González. The complete dialogue is reproduced in Appendix 3 (see page 233-55), courtesy of Carolina González.

"Love in the Time of Aftershocks": This final section of *Red* was originally published as a chapbook, *Love in the Time of Aftershocks* (Santa Cruz, CA: Moving Parts Press and Chusma House Publications, 1998). The following note appears at the end of the chapbook:

> *Love in the Time of Aftershocks* was written in Los Angeles in the time after the 6.7 of January 17, 1994. The chapbook was designed and printed by Felicia

Rice of Moving Parts Press. Co-published by Chusma House Publications and Moving Parts Press on the occasion of "Celebration and Protest," a gathering of poets at La Peña, Berkeley, in support of the author's law suit against the University of California for the denial of tenure, February 12, 1998.

The "6.7 of January 17, 1994," also known as the Northridge earthquake, caused major damage, killing more than sixty and injuring more than nine thousand people. The number 6.7, which precedes this sequence of poems in the text, represents the magnitude of the Northridge quake on the Richter Scale.

Notes for *Frøzen Accident*

"1/3: Derrida and Wittgenstein": Precise identifications of the works by those philosophers Arteaga invokes in this sequence will have to await further study. Meanwhile the references to pensinsula, promontory, and point, here and elsewhere in the book *Frøzen Accident*, suggest allusions to Jacques Derrida's meditations on the destiny of Europe in *L'autre cap*, translated as *The Other Heading: Reflections on Today's Europe*, trans. Pascale-Anne Brault and Michael B. Naas, intro. Michael B. Naas (Bloomington and Indianapolis: Indiana University Press, 1992). The infusion of color throughout this sequence indicates that Arteaga may have had in mind Ludwig Wittgenstein's late *Remarks on Colour*, ed. G. E. M. Anscombe (Berkeley: University of California Press, 1977). Of course, Arteaga's fascination with color permeates his work: see, for example, "Letters of Color" in *Cantos*. It seems probable that Arteaga's use of color throughout *Frøzen Accident* refers in part to pre-Columbian color symbolism, in particular the colors assigned to the cardinal points (red–east, black–north, white–west, and blue/green–south), but that remains to be established.

"3: One Extreme": The poem's "dihydrous oxide" is dihydrogen monoxide, ie. H_2O, or water.

"2/3: Nezahualcoyotl in Mictlan": On Nezahualcoyotl, philosopher king and poet of Tezcoco (elsewhere spelled "Texcoco") in pre-conquest Mexico, see Miguel Léon-Portilla, *Fifteen Poets of the Aztec World* (University of Oklahoma Press, 1992), 70–98. For more about Mictlan, see note above for *Cantos*, "Tercero: El viaje," line 1.

"Field": The poem refers to 122 and 37; San Francisco is located 37.7749° N, 122.4194° W.

"This Point of Hours": See above for the note about "Derrida and Wittgenstein." As for this poem's allusions to "pieces of painted lives" and "the capacity of inks, the red and black, to imagine life," Arteaga commented in an essay: "For the Aztecs and Mexican natives, red and black were both the colors of writing and of existence itself. One vision held that human life was merely played out in the writing of the gods, that we were so much the absent grapheme if without divine articulation." See Alfred Arteaga, "Foreword: The Red and the Black," in *Violence and the Body:*

Race, Gender and the State, ed. Arturo J. Aldama (Bloomington and Indianapolis: Indiana University Press, 2003), viii. See also the poems "Canto of Flight" and "Aristotle."

"Wartezeit für mich, bitte" is German for "(A) pause for me, please."

"Blood Site": The phrase "the near and beside" seems to refer to the Mexican supreme god, Tloque Nahuaque, The Lord of the Close and Near. See León-Portilla, *Fifteen Poets*, 48.

"Canto of Flight": See Nezahualcoyotl's "Song of the Flight," composed during his exile after the assassination of his father Ixtlilxochitl, as mentioned above in the note for "Blood Site." Also see León-Portilla, *Fifteen Poets*, 90–91. Arteaga combines many elements of the pre-Columbian poet's work, rather than solely relying on "Song of the Flight." The word "tlahcuiloco" is probably a compound of Nahuatl "tlahcuilo," scribe or painter of books, and Spanish "loco," crazy. On the tlahcuiloque, see León-Portilla, *Fifteen Poets*, 9. "Equis," in Spanish, is the letter X or "cross"; see the introductory note to *Cantos* on the significance of the X in Xicanx culture and to Arteaga's conception of the poet. "Tochihuitzin Coyolchiuhqui" was a contemporary, ally, and fellow poet of Nezahulacoyotl, and was ruler of Teotlatzinco. See León-Portilla, *Fifteen Poets*, 150–54.

"In Xochitl In Cuicatl": The word "floricanto" in Spanish means flower and song, and translates the diphrasism "in xochitl in cuicatl," the Nahuatl term for poetry. See León-Portilla, *Fifteen Poets*, 54; also see Arteaga's poem "Isla Negra," which follows. "Texcoco Xopan" means Texcoco spring. As noted above, Arteaga spells Texcoco with an "x," León-Portilla with a "z."

"Causeway": A "huipil" is a loose, traditional Mexican Spanish blouse, from the Nahuatl word "huipilli." Arteaga's manuscript notes for this poem indicate that "Xeritzin," which is not a traditional Nahuatl or Aztec name, refers to the Chicana poet and playwright Cherríe Moraga; it is formed from "Xeri" or Cherríe, plus the Nahuatl honorific -tzin, as in Malintzin (the Lady Marina, or La Malinche), or Tonantzin (Reverend Mother).

In the sequence "Nezahualcoyotl in Mictlan," the two guides Gato and Xeritzin echo the traditional Aztec psychopomp Xolotl, with obvious differences. Xolotl, who conducted souls to the afterworld, was thought to be accompanied by a dog, of which the "pale dog" here may be a version. Xeritzin also explicitly resonates with Dante's Virgil (see too the poem "Aristotle"), as Gato does with Charon, the Greek ferryman in Hades. The word "cihuatl" is Nahuatl for woman.

"Mictlan": Tulum is the Mayans' fortified port on the Yucatán peninsula. A "tlamatini," in Nahuatl, is a sage or wise man, keeper of inks and books. See León-Portilla, *Fifteen Poets*, 15.

"Marie Uguay": See the note above for *Cantos*, "Segundo: Textos vivos," line 28. The phrase "son corps est un point fixe" is from Uguay's *L'outre-vie*, 15; "je vous porte dans tes silences historiques" from *L'outre-vie*, 31; and "bercé revêtue / par la blancheur infernale du jour" from *L'outre-vie*, 15. Arteaga's manuscript notes for this poem indicate that "three rivers" may refer to Trois-Rivières, a town in Quebec between Montreal and Quebec City.

"Polylogue": Regarding "Peninsula-tepic": possibly this derives from the Nahuatl "tepic," hard stone.

Notes for *Act Zero*

Since he passed away before the book *Act Zero* could be finalized, Alfred Arteaga never had the opportunity to make any final revisions before this volume went into production. However, the poems were printed in accord with the manuscript he had revised and reviewed.

"Four Portraits in Water": Despite the title, only two poems were ever composed for what may initially have been intended as a quartet.

Notes for Appendix 1: Previously Uncollected Poems

Xochitepec: The plays on the meanings of Nahuatl words in this poem are mostly clear from context. For definitions the reader may also wish to consult the notes for *Cantos* above.

SELECT BIBLIOGRAPHY

Poetic Works by Alfred Arteaga

Arteaga, Alfred. *Act Zero*. Los Angeles: Cusp Books, 2008. Print.

———. *Cantos*. N.p.: Chusma House Publications, 1991. Print.

———. *Frøzen Accident*. Los Angeles: Tia Chucha, 2006. Print.

———. *House with the Blue Bed*. San Francisco: Mercury House, 1997. Print.

———. *Love in the Time of Aftershocks*. Santa Cruz, CA: Moving Parts Press and Chusma House Publications, 1998. (The poems in this chapbook were republished in the book *Red*.)

———. *Red*. Tempe: Bilingual Press/Editorial Bilingüe, 2000. Print.

Critical Works by Alfred Arteaga

Arteaga, Alfred, ed. *An Other Tongue: Nation and Ethnicity in the Linguistic Borderlands*. Durham: Duke University Press, 1994.

———. *Chicano Poetics: Heterotexts and Hybridities*. Cambridge: Cambridge University Press, 1997.

———. *First Words: Origins of the European Nation*. Berkeley: Center for German and European Studies, University of California Press, 1994.

Video Works by Alfred Arteaga

Arteaga, Alfred, dir. *The Present*. 2005. Video poem, 5 minutes.

Arteaga, Alfred, and Yaumaris Leyva Roble, dirs. *Habana Vieja*. 2002. Documentary video, 25 minutes.

Interview

Aldama, Frederick Luis. "Alfred Arteaga." In *Spilling the Beans in Chicanolandia: Conversations with Writers and Artists*. Austin, TX: University of Texas Press, 2010. 53–68.

Selected Critical Works about Alfred Arteaga

Altieri, Charles. "What Is Living and What Is Dead in American Postmodernism: Establishing the Contemporaneity of Some American Poetry." *Critical Inquiry* 22, no. 4 (Summer, 1996): 764–89.

Colón, David. "Other Latino Poetic Method." *Cultural Critique* 47 (Winter, 2001): 265–86.

Hedrick, Tace. "Spik in Glyph? Translation, Wordplay and Resistance in Chicano Bilingual Poetry." *The Translator* 2, no. 2 (1996):141–60.

Perloff, Marjorie. "Logocinema of the Frontiersman: Jolas's Multilingual Poetics and Its Legacies." *Kunapipi* 21 (1999): 145–63.

———. "Postmodernism/Fin de Siecle: The prospects for openness in a decade of closure." *Criticism: A Quarterly for Literature and the Arts* 35, no. 2 (Spring 1993): 161–91.

Urgnani, Elena. "Cicanismo e poesia cicana." *Baldus* 4, nos. 3–4 (1993): 91–98.

———. "L'idea di ibridazzazione in Arteaga e in Voce." *Testuale: critica della poesia contemporanea* 17–18 (1994): 30–40.

Zaccaria, Paola, "Traducir fronteras, poner en escena el transnacionalismo," trans. Marta Company. *De Signis* 12 (2008): 75–84.

A Reader's Companion site containing audio files and other content is available at wesleyan.edu/wespress/readerscompanions

INDEX OF TITLES

INDEX OF FIRST LINES

ABOUT THE CONTRIBUTORS

ALFRED ARTEAGA (1950–2008) was a literary critic and theorist as well as a leading Chicano poet. Born in East Los Angeles, he studied at East Los Angeles College, the University of California, Santa Cruz, and at Columbia University, and he taught at San José City College, the University of Houston, and the University of California, Berkeley. He published six collections of poetry and three critical works, including *Chicano Poetics: Heterotexts and Hybridities* (Cambridge University Press, 1997) and an edited collection of essays, *An Other Tongue: Nation and Ethnicity in the Linguistic Borderlands* (Duke University Press, 1994).

DAVID LLOYD, critic and poet, is Distinguished Professor of English at the University of California, Riverside. His most recent critical book is *Under Representation: The Racial Regime of Aesthetics* (Fordham University Press, 2019). His published poetry includes *Arc & Sill: Poems 1979–2009* (Shearsman Books, 2012), *Bar Null* (SoundEye, 2019), and *Furrow Archive* (Magra Books, 2019).

CHERRÍE MORAGA is a poet, playwright, essayist, and memoirist. Co-editor (with Gloria Anzaldúa) of the anthology *This Bridge Called My Back: Writings by Radical Women of Color* (SUNY Press, fourth edition 2015), she is author of numerous books, including *The Last Generation* (South End Press, 1999), *Loving in the War Years: lo que nunca pasó por sus labios* (South End Press, bilingual edition 2000), *A Xicana Codex of Changing Consciousness: Writings, 2000–2010* (Duke University Press, 2011), and the memoirs *Waiting in the Wings: Portrait of a Queer Motherhood* (Firebrand Books, 1997) and *Native Country of the Heart* (Farrar, Straus and Giroux, 2019).